Structure and Functions of Fantasy

WILEY SERIES ON PERSONALITY PROCESSES

Irving B. Weiner, *Editor*
The University of Rochester Medical Center

Structure and Functions of Fantasy

Eric Klinger

Professor of Psychology
University of Minnesota, Morris

WILEY-INTERSCIENCE   a Division of John Wiley & Sons, Inc
New York · London · Sydney · Toronto

Copyright © 1971, by John Wiley & Sons, Inc.

All rights reserved. Published simultaneously in Canada.

No part of this book may be reproduced by any means, nor transmitted, nor translated into a machine language without the written permission of the publisher.

Library of Congress Catalog Card Number: 78-156331

ISBN 0-471-49125-X

Printed in the United States of America.

10 9 8 7 6 5 4 3 2 1

Series Preface

This series of books is addressed to behavioral scientists concerned with understanding and ameliorating psychological disorders. Its scope should prove pertinent to clinicians and their students in psychology, psychiatry, social work, and other disciplines that deal with problems of human behavior as well as to theoreticians and researchers studying these problems. Although many facets of behavioral science have relevance to psychological disorder, the series concentrates on the three core clinical areas of psychopathology, personality assessment, and psychotherapy.

Each of these clinical areas can be discussed in terms of theoretical foundations that identify directions for further development, empirical data that summarize current knowledge, and practical applications that guide the clinician in his work with patients. The books in this series present scholarly integrations of such theoretical empirical, and practical approaches to clinical concerns. Some pursue the implications of research findings for the validity of alternative theoretical frameworks or for the utility of various modes of clinical practice; others consider the implications of certain conceptual models for lines of research or for the elaboration of clinical methods; and others encompass a wide range of theoretical, research, and practical issues as they pertain to a specific psychological disturbance, assessment technique, or treatment modality.

University of Rochester
Rochester, New York

IRVING B. WEINER

Preface

The writing of this book grew out of an experimental analysis of achievement fantasy. I began the experimental program itself when my difficulties in trying to solve a problem of personality measurement dramatized the inadequacies of theory about responses to projective techniques. Achievement fantasy, probably the most intensively investigated class of projective responses, seemed to be the safest place to begin.

The first results that the program produced were reconcilable with existing notions, but soon our procedures produced data so puzzling, so totally out of keeping with the slender body of theory about projective techniques, that they forced a choice: either abandon the program as producing results that were theoretically inscrutable or pull together a robust enough general theory of fantasy to imbue such unexpected data with theoretical meaning. I chose to theorize.

The project quickly gained its own momentum. Theories of fantasy have, with rare exceptions, remained insulated from general psychology, but much of general psychological theory bears important implications for a theory of fantasy. Knowledge is, after all, of a piece, a nonlinear multidimensional space in which one never knows what he may meet or need next. Fantasy—real-life, free fantasy as well as the processed fragments in projective protocols—partakes of human behavioral organization generally. There were lessons to be extracted from research on play and dreams which have theoretically always been regarded as akin to fantasy; from research on conditioning, imagery, language, and motor skills which reveal aspects of the serial order of response components; and from research on motivation, for the dependence of fantasy content on motivational states is perhaps the best documented relationship concerning fantasy.

· Defined as broadly as it is in this book, "fantasy" encompasses a very large share of waking awareness. Connected, directed thought and concentrated scrutiny of one's environment make up at most a modest fraction of daily life for most people. Even much instrumental thinking goes on interspersed with extraneous elements of thought, and perceptual activity most often takes the form of an automated monitor that coexists with mental activity, much of it fantasy. Fantasy thus contributes much of the inner climate, much of the mental decor, of being human and of being a particular person. However, it is far more than an epiphenomenon; it is, rather, an important part of the human being's system for managing large masses of information. Thus, in this scheme, fantasy is central to human functioning. It is not an encapsulated phenomenon; rather it manifests the operation of processes that enter into a wide variety of nonfantasy responses. Its workings play a critical role in creative thinking. Its organization indicates the need for some modifications of self-theory. Its vicissitudes suggest some conceptual handles for psychotic thought.

Most of the evidence on which this theoretical integration rests was originally gathered for purposes quite unrelated to constructing a theory of fantasy. The original objective of the present effort was, indeed, to synthesize a theory from a great deal of indirect evidence where direct data are scarce, precisely in order to enable investigators to gather more direct data that might be theoretically meaningful. Such a theory would serve little purpose if its conclusions were not affirmative and sometimes even speculative. At the same time, the process of deriving propositions from the available evidence highlights a splendid array of problems for further research.

Writing books of this kind requires time and resources. The National Science Foundation has generously and graciously supported the experimental program and my writing since 1964 through Grants GS-458, GS-1346, and GS-2735. The University of Minnesota contributed toward a research leave in spring quarter, 1967, and a sabbatical leave during 1968–69, both of which I spent in the environments best suited for this work, my home and office in Morris.

The Foundation's support and the generosity of the University of Minnesota, Morris, have made it possible to gather around me an unsurpassable group of people, my undergraduate assistants, who have contributed to all phases of my activity clerically, technically, motivationally, editorially, conceptually, and spiritually. The experimental operations and later the preparation of manuscripts were ably organized and coordinated first by Vernice B. Lehmann (not a student but decidedly a member of the campus community) who set lasting precedents of intelligence, competence, and efficiency, and subsequently by Ronald O. Hietala, Frederick W. McNelly, Jr. (with whom I also collaborated in exploring social role effects on fantasy), and Joseph D. Fridgen. When I most needed freedom to think, they kept our operations going unhampered and shielded me from distraction with equanimity, judgment, and grace. Those others most closely involved with conducting the research cited herein include Romilly W. Cassida, Marjory Hanson, Gene O. Holmblad, Gordon Johnson, Jeri Wine, Barbara

J. Schmidt, Daniel R. Studelska, Jr., and Sharon L. Roerick. A small group who were also involved with conducting experiments came together with me during much of 1970 in a weekly seminar on fantasy: Steven G. Barta, Joseph D. Fridgen, Rachel E. Froiland, and, for a time, Kenneth C. Gregoire and Allan H. Kachelmeier. They have contributed both directly to the manuscript and pervasively through their intellectual stimulation, support, and fellowship. Susan K. Currier completed an editorial run through the manuscript, helping to purge at least some of the stylistic atrocities. The manuscript as a physical entity has passed through several capable hands: Patricia A. Radke, Roxanne M. Anderson, Cheryl A. Brevig, Sandra M. Spillman, and Joyce C. MacIver, the latter two having been caringly involved with it almost throughout its writing.

It would be both futile and impractical to attempt to acknowledge individually all who have exercised an influence on my thinking, even an important influence. Occasionally, however, a debt is too fundamental to go unacknowledged. My decision to become a psychologist owes much to the example, help, and encouragement of Renato Tagiuri, my undergraduate advisor and teacher. I am still discovering the extent to which my thinking has been influenced by Donald W. Fiske. His support, encouragement, and unflappable guidance have sustained me during trying times. This entire manuscript, like many briefer ones before it, has benefited from his unstinting commentaries.

David C. McClelland and Robert C. Birney provided orientation during my initial stages of experimentation on achievement fantasy and have provided encouragement since. They, John W. Atkinson, and Heinz Heckhausen have commented extensively on portions of this and various predecessor manuscripts, forcing me repeatedly to rethink positions and tighten my reasoning.

A number of friends and colleagues have read and commented generously on parts of the manuscript. Irvin Roth has done his best to save me and spare the reader from my worst conceptual excesses. Many others have read sections or chapters and have provided reassurance or significant corrections: Wilfred J. Brogden, George B. Flamer, David Foulkes, Clifton W. Gray, Martin F. Kaplan, Donald C. Norris, Wallace A. Russell, Jerome L. Singer, Theodore E. Uehling, Jr., Hans W. Wendt, and John C. Wright.

For permission to reproduce figures and long quotations I am indebted to the following publishers: American Psychological Association, Dorsey, Hogarth, Macmillan, University of Nebraska Press, and Ronald Press.

Writing a book such as this required a certain kind of nurturance: personal and intellectual freedom, a degree of occupational security, reservation of prejudgments, valuing of creative thrusts, patience with the foibles of unfinished thinking, concern for individual becoming, and the company of interesting people. These priceless qualities, which are by no means the common lot of the young academic, the University of Minnesota, Morris, provided. The campus bears the personal stamp of a remarkable leader, its first dean and provost, Rodney A. Briggs, and the Division of Social Sciences still reflects the enlightened ministrations of its first chairman, now provost, John Q. Imholte. To them and to my faculty and student colleagues who have evolved and maintained the humane traditions of UMM, I am deeply grateful.

My wife Karla has for many years saved me alternately from the worst distractions of a lively family and from irretrievable withdrawal. She created a blend of ready companionship and lofty cuisine that left little else to be desired, and then suffered gamely her reward of watching me lose myself in my work. She contributed to the editing of the entire manuscript. By not remaining the focus of a current concern, she has received less than her share of attention, but for her significance to my life and this book, my gratitude, if I dared express it fully, would be boundless.

Morris, Minnesota   Eric Klinger
April, 1971

Contents

PART I

Introduction

CHAPTER 1

Introduction: Strategy, Definition, History

Consider three snatches of "thought."

1. I want to go out to Colorado. I always said, I always said, I'd go out about the third week in August, but I can't afford to go. I don't know, you know, the mountains out there well, I, free, isn't the, the right word that I want. It just makes me feel so by myself, like there is no one else around me, like I couldn't care, I, I just couldn't care if anybody else ever came close to me again, and just, I could feel up in those mountains and watching trees blow and and just up there by yourself. Ha. It's really something, just like lying on the beach . . . big beach. Drown my sorrows out. Be happy reach out and cry. Cry, seems so hard to cry. I have things to cry over, but the tears aren't, just don't come. Tears. I'm emotional, but I'm not that emotional.

2. I'm getting hungry. My stomach is starting growling just like it was in church last Sunday. Oh, I was so embarrassed. Fell asleep in church sitting in the front row. Not in the front row exactly but it was the front row of people. What a night before though. Out to four o'clock in the morning and she was out till five I guess. I left before she did from the party. Albright State Park. What a park! Nothing but a river. Drinking beer, and then I fall asleep in church. I guess that that isn't showing much is it? I should be ashamed of myself. I am. I got to stop drinking though. I've—ouch—I got to stop biting my fingernails too. Wish I'd get a date one of these days. Such a coward—never ask anyone. Maybe nobody would go with me anyway. I guess that's my problem. Got a defeatist attitude before I even start.

3. Almost time for that old biology. Gotta go to English today too. I wanted to skip it but he's assigning a theme. I hate those themes. I really, I only got four left now. Written themes until they're coming out of my ears. Think I'll, the rain is kinda nice. Never really noticed it that much before. When I go home tonight I think I'm going to take out a girl I know that's in high school from my home town. Take her over to the play. I've got tickets to the play tonight—Viet Rock. I don't know, I've read a few things about the guy that wrote this play. About, in the paper, about, about why he wrote.

All three passages are excerpts from longer transcripts produced by college students, in these instances a woman and two men, who were asked to do nothing but "think out loud." The passages have one feature in common: none contain concerted efforts to solve problems. For that reason, they fall outside the purview of all major, modern theories of "thinking." Yet, after duly allowing for the fact that the subjects knew they were communicating with an experimenter, these excerpts exemplify the kind of mental activity that occupies a very large portion of waking life, for instance while resting, while waiting for something with little else to do, while performing routine actions on a job or at home, while walking or driving, while going to sleep or waking up, and, seemingly, interspersed among nearly all other kinds of activity as well. Much of what people know about themselves they experience in this form. The process infuses the feeling of being human. In the usage of this book, it is the sort of activity denoted by the term "fantasy."

The examples of fantasy that are reproduced above seem mundane, but in this regard they seem typical of normal waking fantasy. Vivid, dramatic daydreams also often occur, of course, and when fantasies are completely private they are no doubt often saltier than these, but there is reason to believe that the average human's average fantasy is, in fact, somewhat humdrum. Some fantasies are extremely enjoyable. Others are filled with sorrow or fear. Many others feel emotionally unremarkable, if not quite neutral. Because they characterize so large a part of human inner experience, however, the process of which they are part seems intrinsically interesting.

Fantasy also carries important implications from the standpoint of behavioral science. The structure of so common an activity most probably carries profound significance for the organization of human behavior generally. Furthermore, in a species that has evolved through such an extended molding by natural selection, so prominent an activity as fantasy is likely to exercise important functions in the adaptation of the organism. This book, therefore, embarks on a search for the structure and functions of fantasy.

After millennia of philosophical inquiry into mind, a half century of experimental analysis of consciousness, and a further half century of experimental analysis of behavior, very little is actually known about fantasy. There are many reasons for our ignorance. Western civilization, for example, has long placed the highest value on active, willed reason rather than on the interstitial fantasy that forms the matrix for reasoned thought. Indeed, the West is oriented toward action outward, not toward contemplation of inner experience. Furthermore, science and psychology have historically developed in such a way as to channel scientific efforts around instead of into the investigation of fantasy, and have inhibited the search for appropriate methods.

In recent years the investigator interested in fantasy has found himself in a quandary. On the one hand he has been hampered in the collection of data by the lack of well-specified theory from which to deduce hypotheses. In some sense all rigorously obtained data have potential value, but their meaningfulness to science and the scientist at the time of their collection depends to some extent on the existing state of relevant theory. On the other hand in the absence of good data theory-building is hazardous and frustrating. Hence the dearth of well-specified theory and of rigorous, pertinent data exercise a reciprocally inhibiting influence on each other. To escape the quandary thus requires either epochal patience or a detour.

The strategy of detour that guides this book assumes optimistically that the science contains more information relevant to a theory of fantasy than has been apparent. The information arises from the maturing investigations of fantasy-*like* processes and of phenomena so basic to all psychological functioning that their rich implications for fantasy can constitute the scaffolding and materials of a comprehensive theory of fantasy as such.

Any attempt to construct a theory of fantasy must face a number of critical preliminary decisions. What kind of theory shall it be? How shall the basic phenomenon be defined? What epistemological constraints must the theory observe to retain its scientific legitimacy?

WHAT KIND OF THEORY?

Fantasy as conceived here is a process quite central to normal human functioning. A theory of fantasy must therefore be concerned with the properties of fantasy as a process—of what it consists, the conditions under which it occurs, how it unfolds in time, its relationships to other organismic processes, its sources of energy and direction, and the functions it performs in human adaptation.

No doubt fantasy processes, like all biological properties, vary among individuals; and the study of individual differences can provide valuable information concerning the phenomenon. Nevertheless, the proposed theory is not primarily differential. First, useful differential data can be integrated into a process-oriented theory; second, an excellent summary of existing differential as well as developmental data is already available (Singer, 1966).

The form of the theory is verbal and discursive rather than mathematical and parametric. However, the theory is stated in terms which are either roughly quantitative or readily quantifiable. All of the theoretical assertions are intended to be fully testable, at least in principle.

DEFINING FANTASY

Definition and Theory

The definition of a phenomenon is often inseparable in scientific work from theory about the phenomenon; for instance, the decision to study the cell structure of a particular animal species presupposes that organisms can be divided meaningfully into cells, and that supposition in turn rests on a theory of tissue structure. In the same way, the study of a particular chemical element makes sense only insofar as the element is thought to constitute a scientifically useful class of phenomena, and that judgment in turn rests on an elaborate body of prior data and theory. Lavoisier's reformulation of chemical theory sprang from his attempt to revise chemical nomenclature (Toulmin, 1969). No one today would argue against the usefulness of cells and elements as ways of describing biological structures and chemical substances, because the use of these classes has resulted in massive advances in their respective sciences.

The case of fantasy is quite different. There is no set of generally accepted criteria for discerning the boundaries of fantasy. Most investigators would agree that a fictional tale created by a subject for his own pleasure and for no further purpose constitutes an instance of fantasy. However, few such pure instances occur. Creating tales in inner experience shades into laying plans, reminiscing, analyzing past events, anticipating future ones, asking oneself questions, engaging in brief reflections, entertaining disorganized imagery, and, in bed, experiencing night dreams. No one pretends to know just where fantasy leaves off and adjacent processes begin. Many investigators have attempted other terminology. Some have proposed to limit themselves to "daydreams," but while "daydreams" may seem to offer boundaries less farflung than "fantasy," the boundaries are no clearer, and there is little added assurance that the phenomena called "daydreams" are more coherent as a class than those called "fantasy." Antrobus (1969) has focused on "stimulus-independent thought," but this includes instrumental thought concerning situations in the past or future. Thus there have been numerous studies of "fantasy" and "daydreams," and some of "stimulus-independent thought," but the studies are concerned with sometimes quite divergent phenomena.

Yet differences exist between fantasy experiences and other internal events. Few people would respond to a car rushing at them at high speed by resorting to fantasy, and few people have not spent some of their leisure time imagining how it would be for them in some imaginary situation that alters present realities. Mental work and daydreaming feel subjectively quite different. As responses they occur with different frequency in different situations, and many writers have detected that both serve useful but different functions. Psychologically, when different states feel different, they are different. The differences need not be reflected in the various behavioral measures of human performance, although we see that in fact they are. States that feel different produce differences that can at least be detected by the external observer in verbal behavior when subjects report how they feel.

A Working Definition of Fantasy

Despite the present state of confusion about the definition of fantasy, any investigation of fantasy must have some starting point, at least a working definition. Such a definition should encompass the phenomenon of fantasy not only conceptually but also operationally, or at least provide means for employing operations to distinguish it from other forms of activity.

One obvious defining property of fantasy is that it is primarily a mental activity, not a gross motor behavior, and is therefore necessarily covert. In the existing state of research methods, however, ideational processes are too complex and elusive to be measured directly. Some day psychology may have psychophysiological methods that can provide enough information about covert processes to permit the measurement of their structure and content, but that day is still far off. Meanwhile, studies of fantasy must rely on subjects' overt behavior to report on their fantasies, and at least part of the overt behavior must be subjects' verbal reports on their inner experiences.

From the standpoint of defining fantasy operationally, the purely mentalistic definition of fantasy proposed by English and English (1958) provides little help: "Imagining a complex object or event in concrete symbols as images, whether or not the object or event exists; or the symbols or images themselves: for example, a daydream." Furthermore, the definition seems not to exclude some kinds of directed thought that might also employ "concrete symbols as images."

Considerably more helpful is Singer's (1966) attempt to define "daydreaming." Amid several paragraphs of partial definitions, synonyms, and examples, Singer wrote that daydreaming "is used to mean a shift of attention away from an ongoing physical or mental task or from a perceptual response to external stimulation towards a response to some internal stimulus [p. 3]." Taken as a definition, the statement suggests some ways of measuring fantasy. Recent work on attention, for example, has developed to the point where shifts in attention might be expected to show up in eye movements, detection errors, and other such behavioral indicators. Some investigations have already begun to relate such measures to subjects' self-reports of fantasy (Singer, 1966), but their status as adequate operational definitions of fantasy is still much in doubt.

The Singer definition leaves some other problems as well; for instance, it seems possible for people to perform physical tasks at least somewhat attentively while still engaging in snatches of fantasy. Consider the following monologue by a subject "thinking out loud" while solving wire puzzles that required him to separate two twisted lengths of rigid, heavy-guage wire:

> I've never been able to work these kinds of puzzles before. I probably won't get any of them before five minutes are up. (Pause) There we go, I got one. So, go on to the next one. Let's see, these things (Pause). They seem to be so easy but yet so hard and actually they're not, they're easy if you just know what to do but it's more or less a guess game, I guess. (Pause) I used to work with these all the time or not all the time—once in awhile. I got some from my folks but I never enjoyed doing it much. I don't know if I enjoy doing it now either. I've never had them in a test before. When the girl first called she said I was supposed, asked if I wanted to be in an experiment. I thought she was pulling a joke, but I guess it isn't. My roommate took this too, this experiment, and he was telling me that. I'm going on to the next puzzle.

Clearly, much of his verbalization was not directed at the solution of the puzzles, but the puzzle-solving continued with the subject's attention ostensibly focused on it during the entire interval. The concept of "attention" can in this context be quite slippery.

One is left also with the problem of differentiating verbal reports of task-directed ideation from reports of fantasy ideation. Many statements in the samples of "thinking out loud" that are supposed to illustrate fantasy are, in fact, statements about problems in the subjects' lives. In the course of fantasy, they often feel different and seem to serve a different function than they do in problem-solving thought. How make the distinction?

One basis for distinguishing is suggested by comparing the samples of "thinking out loud" that began the chapter with the following purely problem-directed excerpt reported by a subject while trying to solve a verbal logic problem:

> Three white hats and two red hats. It would be a red and a white and a red and a white. *Holy buckets. I never understand these things. All right now,* if the first guy thinks he isn't going to say either one because he has got a red and one has got a white. The next guy says the same thing because one has got a red and one had got a white so that means it would have to be a white hat, *I think. Sure, wouldn't it?* I can clearly see that my hat is white because if two and three had red and white and then he turned around and (inaud) he had a red and white. *Yeah,* it would probably be white. *I don't know.* I never was very bright.

The italicized portions of the excerpt all have one feature in common, an evaluation of the validity of the ideational process itself. Other subjects who felt more successful in the successive stages of solving the problems peppered the protocol with an "OK" following the completion of each step. The fantasy samples also contained evaluative statements, but the evaluations were of objects, events or past actions, not of the success of current problem-solving steps. This distinction thus provides a means whereby a content analyst can separate "fantasy" from "nonfantasy" passages.

There is still another potential means for distinguishing fantasy from directed thought. During problem-solving, subjects have a sense of "trying" to achieve some result by means of their ideation. It is a more or less concerted, volitional process, involving more or less sense of effort. Fantasy, on the other hand, normally feels spontaneous, except when in artificial situations the fantasy is deliberately intended to create an effect. The phenomenological difference is elusive conceptually, but most likely quite important theoretically. Given the uncertain, unanchored nature of all knowledge, both behavioral and phenomenological (Campbell, 1969), it would be rash to discard this kind of information while investigating so imperfectly charted a matter as fantasy. Whether the behaviorist and phenomenological indicators of fantasy actually converge on the same process is at least partly a matter for future empirical investigation.

To summarize the case up to this point, then, fantasy is covert, must at this time be investigated largely by relying on subjects' verbal reports of their ideation, and involves ideation other than that required directly to perform present tasks. Furthermore, the kind of ideation that qualifies as instrumental to performing a task is marked by subjects' tendency to evaluate the ideation itself for its usefulness in advancing them toward an objective, and subjects feel as though they are trying.

If a definition of fantasy is to rest on these ideas, then the definition must be stated negatively as lacking certain properties of instrumental, task-performing activities. Negative definitions are inherently unsatisfactory for theoretical purposes because one can never be sure that one has excluded all of the elements one wishes to exclude, and the definition remains theoretically somewhat unassertive. However, lack of theoretical commitment is desirable at this early stage, since it avoids too greatly constraining the theoretical development which the definition is intended to foster. In any case scientific taxonomies depend on the state of relevant knowledge, and the relevant behavioral domain has simply been insufficiently mapped to support the setting of rigorous positive boundaries on the concept of fantasy.

Accordingly, for present purposes, fantasy is defined as verbal reports of all mentation whose ideational products are not evaluated by the subject in terms of their usefulness in advancing some immediate goal extrinsic to the mentation itself; that is, fantasy is defined as report of mentation other than orienting responses to, or scanning of, external stimuli, or operant activity such as problem-solving in a task situation.

The definition ventured here includes reports of daydreams, reverie, or musing while listening to Beethoven, but excludes reading, ideation during moments of fright while narrowly avoiding an accident, or the inspection of graffiti. It includes a daydream about the possible course of a future interview, but it excludes a planning session on how to conduct it.

Obviously, the definition leaves some boundary ambiguities and depends for its operational adequacy entirely on the highly questionable veridicality of verbal self-reports, but it mirrors the present state of knowledge in the field and seems sufficiently workable to communicate the topic of the book.

A CAPSULE HISTORY

The study of fantasy, now as always, is necessarily caught up in the web of historical forces: *Zeitgeist, Ortgeist,* and the development of epistemology. It seems desirable, therefore, before embarking on a consideration of the phenomenon itself, to place the inquiry in context.

The Moratorium on the Study of Inner Experience

Our relative ignorance of fantasy arises out of an historical moratorium on the investigation of inner experience, especially in the United States, approximately from 1920 until 1960. The behavioristic and neobehavioristic tide that swept academic departments of psychology during these 40 years transformed psychological science and produced some stunning advances in psychological knowledge. One of the costs was the relative neglect of some classical psychological problems, not the least of which was the description of inner experience.

The systematic exploration of inner experience received a major impetus in the West from Saint Augustine (Windelband, 1901), who made the self-evident validity of inner experience the cornerstone of his philosophy and, thenceforth, the cornerstone of Christian epistemology. If man's knowledge of himself serves as his guide to his knowledge of God, then man's knowledge of his inner experience becomes a supremely important subject for investigation. Augustine's doctrines eventually exerted a profound influence on the form of Christian philosophy, but the philosophic tradition that succeeded him turned its attention for seven centuries primarily to the elaboration of the tools of Aristotelian logic and to the controversy between the realists and the nominalists over the reality of individual entities. Scientific inquiry into the nature of inner experience was still far in the future. The 12th century philosopher, John of Salisbury, outlined a description of the categories of inner experience and applied the unifying associative principle expounded earlier by Aristotle, that ideas experienced contiguously come to be linked in future thought. Like Augustine, he assigned importance to the role of volition in directing thought. Thomas Hobbes grasped the threads of this embryonic psychology and wove them into a systematic account of individual experience and social behavior. He also began the placement of psychology in the empirical tradition that was gathering momentum in the natural sciences of the seventeenth century. He wrote in *Leviathan* (1651), "Whosoever looks into himself and considers what he does when he does *think, opine, reason, hope, fear,* etc., and upon what grounds, he shall thereby read and know what are the thoughts and passions of all other men upon the like occasions [p. 24]." Thus began the work of the British associationist school of psychology, whose development through men like Locke, Hume, Hartley, the Mills, and Brown led to a psychology late in the 19th century that applied increasingly sophisticated observational techniques, which have been called in retrospect "introspective," to the psychological study of inner events.

The diverse introspective psychologies that flourished at the turn of the century declined under the pressure of several developments, some external and some internal. American psychology was rapidly gaining in vigor, and its spirit reflected the pragmatic qualities of its society. American psychologists accordingly turned their attention most vigorously to the study of individual differences among men, following the path made in Britain by Galton, or to the role that various aspects of mental life play in the efficient functioning of the organism, or to the psychology of animals. All three kinds of preoccupation focus on behavioral variables, and they are easily related to the powerful theoretical system that grew out of Darwinism. They stood in sharp contrast to the psychology of the structure of mental content, whose major representative in America, E. B. Titchener, was an Englishman trained in Germany and "never became a part of American psychology [Boring, 1950, p. 413]." American psychology eventually lost patience with the structuralist approaches of Wundt, Titchener, and the various introspectionist countermovements when the internal requirements of the introspectionist research led them to a methodological impasse. The very success of the introspectionist psychologists in formulating increasingly precise and revealing questions placed increasing demands on the observational and judgmental capacities of their highly trained observer-subjects. Eventually, the demands proved too great, and the methods then available for the further empirical investigation of inner experience were shown to be inadequate.

The scope of the reaction, however, far exceeded the difficulties with methodology. American psychologists not only rejected introspective methods, but also the inner events that they believed could then only be investigated introspectively. They took the occasion to declare their total independence from philosophical concerns other than the philosophy of science. They redefined psychology; James' "Science of Mental Life" became Watson's "science of behavior." They brought powerful methods of quantitative description and analysis to bear on the new behavioral data. Watson's 1913 program for psychology called for a reformulation of most of the traditional problems of psychological investigation in behaviorist terms, but he conceded that other problems would have to be neglected.

The phenomena of fantasy were prominently among those chosen for neglect. Until 1966, not a single book was published in the United States that devoted itself wholly to the systematic examination of fantasy, under whatever name. Few books appeared in other countries, and these partook in varying degrees of the advances in Western psychological theory and method. Long's *Collected Papers on the Psychology of Phantasy,* which appeared in Britain in 1921, is much more an exposition of Jungian analytic psychology than a systematic treatment of fantasy. Varendonck applied a curious blend of introspective methods and early psychoanalytic theory to his own fantasy experiences in his *Psychology of Daydreams* (1921). The result was an extensive exploration of rich data, which yielded insights and conclusions that ought to have been heuristically provocative, but were largely ignored. Varendonck's methods were, to be sure, wholly unsatisfactory by contemporary standards, but in the intervening half century no one has come to grips directly with the problems posed by Varendonck with methods more satisfactory than his. Green's *The Daydream* (1923) attempted to trace developmental stages of daydreaming. The theoretical framework is psychoanalytic and the evidence is anecdotal. Sartre's *Psychology of Imagination* (1965) is a phenomenological and philosophical analysis of the nature of consciousness. Rapaport brought together a large and valuable collection of periodical articles and book excerpts in his *Organization and Pathology of Thought* (1951). The selections draw on prebehavioristic introspectionists such as Narziss Ach, Gestaltists such as Lewin, and a large number of psychoanalytic writers. The ratio of theory to data was dizzyingly high, and the theory was based at best on acute clinical observation. McKellar (1957) has selectively reviewed work on imagery, fantasy-like thought, and their application to thinking, particularly creative thinking. In 1966, Singer published *Daydreaming,* the first American work devoted exclusively to the psychological examination of fantasy, and the first Western work of this kind since Varendonck's.

Thus, in the mid-1960's, the moratorium came to an end. Indeed, in 1960, Hebb noted the readiness for change and called for a "second phase" of the American Behaviorist Revolution that might readdress itself to neglected problems. Silvan Tomkins about the same time launched an effort to advance both theory and experimentation on "affects." The 1967 Annual Convention of the American Psychological Association was dedicated to "The Unfinished Business of William James," and the 1968 Convention sported a symposium, among others, entitled "Whatever Happened to the Will in American Psychology?" and a paper entitled "The Ecology of Consciousness." Clearly, the wheel had turned.

Research on Fantasy-Like Processes

It would be a mistake to suppose that the period of the moratorium was completely sterile for a theory of fantasy. The period was one of great expansion in psychological research, both in quantity of output and in the production of new research problems and techniques. Investigations by both academic and clinical psychologists produced results in several areas that border on the area of fantasy. Investigations of free play continued into the 1930's and investigations of doll play and other projective techniques mushroomed from the 1930's to the 1950's, including the Rorschach inkblot test, the Thematic Apperception Test (TAT), the various drawing tests, sentence completion tests, and hundreds of lesser-known instruments. Studies of psychotic language and of dreaming gained both momentum and rigor during the 1950's and 1960's. Problems of associative structure, learning, and integration continued throughout the period, and the 1950's saw the initiation of significant movements in psycholinguistics and computer simulation of thought processes. The same decade gave rise to direct investigations of creative thinking and stimulus-seeking behavior.

While none of these many lines of inquiry bore directly on the nature of free fantasy, all of them produced ideas and data having indirect relevance. Therefore, one major purpose of this volume is to weave the relevant strands into an integrated, testable theory of fantasy.

THE PLAN OF THE BOOK

The two kinds of phenomena that have traditionally been considered most fantasy-like are play and dreams. Each has received considerable scrutiny as a process, far more fully than comparable process investigations of free fantasy. Chapters 2 and 3 of Part II accordingly review data and theories that bear on the processes of play and dreams with an eye to their implications for a theory of fantasy. The winnowing procedure necessarily also constitutes a parallel review of relevant process studies of fantasy.

If fantasy is to be examined as a process—and a response process at that—it may be expected to share the properties of other response processes. Presumably all behavioral sequences display some sort of episodic or segmental organization over time, partake of certain common switching or linking mechanisms between segments, contain certain intrasegmental organizing principles, and reflect the effects of concurrent organismic states of certain kinds. Chapters 4 through 7 of Part III examine the way in which these basic behavioral attributes might characterize fantasy, and draw conclusions for the structure of fantasy and its functional role in adaptation.

Parts II and III, then, provide a theoretical framework within which to view existing and prospective data of fantasy. They only skim some accumulated information concerning the effects on fantasy content of two classes of antecedent events: motive states and stimulus events. Most of the data arise from studies that employ projective techniques rather than measures of free fantasy, but the design of these studies nevertheless appears to permit some useful inferences. Chapters 8 to 12 of Part IV review the material of motivational and stimulus effects on fantasy.

The theoretical development in Chapters 2 through 12 emerges in the course of examining a mixed bag of data and theories, and it is therefore somewhat dispersed. Chapter 13 provides a discursive summary of the book that may also usefully be read as an overview before proceeding to Chapters 2 through 12. The appendix further integrates and recasts the theory in a propositional form intended both to summarize the state of knowledge with respect to the major features of the theory and to facilitate the process of testing and revising or extending it.

CHAPTER 2

Implications of Play for a Theory of Fantasy*

The subject of free fantasy has been conspicuously neglected by scientific psychologists during the last forty years. So, to some extent, has play. Play is a behavioral phenomenon, however, easier to observe and record, and easier to relate to the main body of behavior theory and neobehaviorism. Accordingly, while well-focused, comprehensive, rigorous observational studies of play are rare, some direct observational studies exist, and there is much indirect observation and theory that have been brought to bear on the phenomenon. Whereas the available empirical studies of fantasy have largely been concerned with correlational data and individual differences, empirical studies of play, while often methodologically crude, have attempted in larger proportion to examine the structure of play and its antecedent-consequent relationships.

The validity of generalizing from evidence on play to a theory of fantasy depends on the proposition that the two psychological processes are highly related, and that for at least some limited purposes the one may stand as an analogue for the other. This is the first proposition that must be examined, following the establishment of some definitions. Then it will be possible to review further some of the attributes of play and assess their implications for theories of fantasy.

DEFINITIONS OF PLAY

Play

Nearly everyone feels he understands what is meant by "play," and investigators are even able substantially to agree in identifying particular in-

---

* An earlier version of this chapter has appeared in article form (Klinger, 1969). The copyright (1969) is held by the American Psychological Association, Inc. Reproduced by permission.

dreams as organized around a motivational structure of wishes. The tenability of this aspect of the theory depended upon highly complex inferences, the rules for which were ill-defined. Recent evidence has led numerous experimenters (e.g., Foulkes, 1966; Murray, 1965) to reject wish-fulfillment as a law of dreaming, but it fails to rule out the law of wish-instigation of dreams. However, since the evidence for the theory was anecdotal and clinical, and not the result of experimental analysis, "wish" could escape operational definition and was subject to confounding with other variables.

One such variable is an individual's emotional involvement in an unconsummated instrumental response sequence or an unrealized imminent event. For purposes of brevity, this variable is referred to as "current concerns." The vulnerability of the wish and current-concerns variables to mutual confounding seems evident, in that interrupted response sequences and emotionally involving, imminent events entail goals, expectations of pleasure or pain, and, presumably, wishes. The advantages of the emotional involvement variable, which make it worthy of examination, are (a) readier operational definition, (b) a requirement of less complex symbolic interpretation of dreams, and (c) the capacity for ready articulation with contemporary behavior theory.

It is not the primary purpose of the present section to attempt the Herculean task of reconstructing dream theory; but in order to draw implications from dream data for a theory of fantasy, the dream data must first be interpreted. What follows is an attempt to show that the position is consistent with what is known of reasonably well-understood dreams and to indicate its potential relationships with behavioral and neobehaviorist concepts.

In regard to the compatibility of the current-concerns variable with what is known of dreams, useable evidence is relatively scarce simply because the contexts of published dreams were not analyzed with this variable in mind and because experimentally obtained dreams are usually altogether unanalyzed with respect to context. However, a relatively small sample will suffice to make the point, which is that the effective "day residues" that determine dreams are more than simply occurrences; they are emotionally laden events that have yet to run their course.

Turning, for example, to those of Freud's (1900) dreams that are presented in sufficient relevant detail to suit present purposes, one finds that all appear to permit such an interpretation. Thus the dream about his patient Irma (pp. 106–121) was preceded a few hours earlier by a friend having aroused Freud's concern about her therapeutic progress enough to mobilize him to formulate her case history for submission to a consultant; and it was clear that Freud's anxiety about his therapeutic program for her and its effects on his family relationships were not fully assuaged by this effort. Freud's "yellow beard" dream (pp. 136–141) was occasioned the evening before by the visit of a friend who both aroused Freud's concern regarding a university appointment and indicated an obstacle in the way of Freud's receiving it. Again, the issue remained very much alive. Similarly, the five of Freud's six examples of dreams instigated by "recent and indifferent material" (pp. 165–173) that include sufficient contextual detail can be traced to the elicitation on the previous day of a response sequence or expectancy of significant emotional valence; for example, his dream of seeing before him a monograph he had written on a certain plant seems to be traceable to his desire to finish his real book on dreams, of which he was reminded on the day before by a letter from his friend Fliess and by meeting one of the authors of a *Festschrift* that incorporated the achievements of his colleagues. By coincidence he had also that morning seen a botanical monograph in a shop window. Freud's associations to this dream make clear that these events both elicitied memories of his earlier failures in botany and mobilized attempts to bolster his self-esteem by dwelling on his success in studying the pharmacology of the coca plant. Thus the probable instigators were more than mere occurrences; they set in motion a cluster of fears and blame-avoidant responses to deny failure and get on with his real tasks, which remained uncompleted at bed-time.

Similar evidence that current concerns influence dream content has been provided by Rechtschaffen, Vogel, and Shaikun (1963), who awoke subjects during both REM and NREM periods and analyzed the manifest content of each subject's dreams for interrelatedness. They produced several examples of recurrent dream content relevant to subjects' current activities which either were still in progress (e.g., planning a camping trip or finishing a term paper) or were probably short of their final consequence (having just finished final examinations). Rechtschaffen et al. concluded that "manifest elements tend to be repeated during a night on occasions when preoccupations of the recent past remain so intense that they 'press' for discharge throughout the sleep period [p. 546]." In the same vein, Whitman, Pierce, Maas, and Baldridge (1962) report that subjects in a sleep laboratory experience an artificially high incidence of dreams concerning the laboratory situation, and Dement, Kahn, and Roffwarg (1965) found the incidence of dreams about the laboratory situation to decline on successive nights as the subject adapts to the experimental procedure. One way to define a current concern operationally is to prevent subjects from engaging in activities they would normally choose. Wood (1962) placed five subjects in social isolation for an entire day. He reported that on the following night his subjects experienced an upsurge in social-interaction dreams.

The first part of the present hypothesis, that dream content is determined by current concerns, thus seems consistent with available evidence. There is a second aspect of the position, however, to the effect that dream content does not simply reflect other presleep occurrences, such as sheer activity of a certain kind. Some evidence is available to support this assertion. Hauri (1966) had subjects engage in six-hour periods of physical exercise, study, or relaxation immediately prior to sleep. His subjects were *less* inclined to dream of physical activity after exercise than after study or relaxation. There is partial evidence that this inverse relationship reflected the mobilization of a current concern, since the design forced subjects to bed immediately after exercise, and some subjects attempted unsuccessfully to interpose a period of waking activity other than exercise before going to sleep. Subjects' REM dreams also contained less problem-solving activity after study, but their NREM dreams contained slightly more. It is difficult to interpret this result. However, several of the subjects were students under considerable pressure to study. It seems possible that the six-hour exercise and relaxation periods constituted a serious interruption in their goal-striving activity and led to heightened problem-solving dreams during the more emotional REM periods. Thus even sustained, unusual activity as such seems not to produce corresponding dream content, but the evidence is consistent with the interpretation that it may affect dream content through the mobilization of current concerns. The ineffectiveness of sheer presleep experiences also receives confirmation from the evidence of Foulkes and Rechtschaffen (1964) that the content of films seen just before bedtime, whether violent or not, was rarely incorporated into subsequent dreams.

The Instigating Mechanism

Accepting the role of current concerns as dream instigators may seem no more helpful than accepting interests or wishes for purposes of solving one important problem, namely the determination of the specific timing and sequencing of dream segments. A concern, like an interest or a need-based wish, presumably remains relatively constant throughout a given night and therefore provides no basis for predicting that relevant dreams should occur at particular moments. It is, indeed, true that all of these variables require a further mechanism to make them operative, but the advantage of the current-concerns variable lies in its greater adaptability to known mechanisms.

The brief discussion that follows is included here to indicate the nature and outlines of a proposed associative mechanism, whose plausibility strengthens the argument that a "current concerns" variable provides a useful cog in the theoretical machinery for explaining the structure of dreaming. The discussion anticipates several later chapters, to which its elaboration and substantiation are deferred.

Many previous writers have proposed an associative mechanism for ordering the bits of potential dream content. An associative unfolding that gradually incorporates relevant day residues and interests seems to satisfy many of the requirements of an acceptable mechanism, but general formulations have often seemed attractive because of their ambiguity, while they fail to specify what they are primarily supposed to provide: the particular kind of associative linkage between bits of content. Freud, like others, rejected the naive associationism of his day as an acceptable theory of dream instigation. The more recent evidence that dream elements may recur during a given night without ever duplicating their associations or contexts (Dement and Wolpert, 1958b; Rechtschaffen, Vogel, and Shaikun, 1963) also appears to rule out a naive associationism; but, after all, since understanding of associative processes has matured considerably in the past 70 years, a more refined associative explanation need not be dismissed out of hand.

A useful further specification of the mechanism is possible if we consider, first, the properties of the ideational stream during sleep, and, second, the nature of a "current concern."

Insofar as the dream-like ideation is understood it seems certain to be characterized at least by topical drift. Dream ideation is not systematic— at least, not by the rules of directed thought—and is apparently continually diverted. Its topical instability is apparent not only from dream sample to dream sample, but even within a particular dream sample. The direction of drift is not readily predictable from the usual principles of word-association (although those principles have not been applied systematically to dream data) and higher order associative principles seem restricted to operant kinds of activity and therefore appear inapplicable to dream data. The question of associative principles as they bear on fantasy processes are considered more fully in Chapters 6 and 7.

"Current concerns" were defined as operant response sequences that remained unconsummated either because the sequence had been interrupted or because the consequence had not yet taken place, but which had not yet been abandoned; and the consequence was assumed to be important to the individual—that is, capable of stirring strong emotions. Under these circumstances, it may be presumed from general psychological theory that instrumental responses relevant to the sequence will remain for a time after interruption high in the individual's response hierarchy, that relevant sets will remain easily elicited, and that relevant associations will be well primed. In conjunction with this potentiation of responses, the present position accepts the general conclusion of two writers working within quite different frameworks (Mowrer, 1960; Tomkins, 1962) that behavior is organized around affective responses; and it therefore seems reasonable to suppose also that the affective responses relevant to an unconsummated response sequence will also be easily elicited and may, in fact, form a context for the elicitation of the remaining relevant responses.

Within the conceptual framework sketched above, it is now necessary only to picture the situation of the sleeper, who is thinking or dreaming of a particular event. His flow of images, including verbal images, acts as a set of cues which in turn elicit new responses. Indeed, Freud (1900) has observed that "In the case of two consecutive dreams it can often be observed that one takes as its central point something that is only on the periphery of the other, and *vice versa* . . . [p. 525]." The evidence reviewed earlier that dream content is influenced by current concerns suggests that the determination of which peripheral element of an existent dream sequence will form the central point of the next depends on which element is associated with the strongest current concern and hence yields the strongest new affective response.

In view of the mechanism sketched above, it is now necessary to qualify the position that dream content is determined by current concerns. The more fundamental prediction from this model is that the direction of dream flow depends on which element has the ability to arouse an affective response conditioned to it powerfully enough to mobilize a new sequence of ideational responses. As an important special case, it is hypothesized that current concerns potentiate relevant affective and other responses and are therefore likely to dominate the flow of serial arousals. However, the continual successive arousals of less powerful affective responses will produce a continual shifting of nuances and symbolic constructions.

The model suggests that dream segments are serially elicited in a sequence of respondent responses, in Skinner's sense of "respondent" to contrast with "operant": elicited, not emitted; and controlled by antecedents, not consequences. In dreams the respondent quality seems especially prominent and is consistent with Hartmann's (1967) conclusion that dream sequences feel involuntary, in the sense that they are experienced as beyond the individual's power to exercise free will.

The proposed model of an instigating mechanism accomplishes the task of reconciling a dream determinant that is relatively constant for a given night with the observable facts that the dreams of a single night are highly heterogeneous and that the effect of any determinant can be observed at best recurrently. The model at this point leaves unspecified the structure of the dream segments themselves, with respect to both their organization and their symbolic properties.

Affective Arousal During Dream Sequences

The proposed model for dream instigation is intended to be fully testable. One of its prominent features is the role of conditioned affective arousal in determining the transition from one dream segment to the next. The model permits the affective response to be minor, but, in principle, it must be somehow detectable. The present section reviews existing evidence for the affective aspect of the instigating mechanism.

The Experience of Affect in Dreams. Dreams do, of course, frequently contain affective experiences as a part of their content. Freud (1900) recognized their presence, but also pointed out that the portrayal of affect in dreams is quite variable. On the one hand, he wrote, "A dominating element in a sleeper's mind may be constituted by what we call a 'mood'—or *tendency* to some affect—and this may then have a determining influence upon his dreams. . . . [I]t will be accompanied by the trains of thought appropriate to it [p. 487]." On the other hand, he wrote,

The detachment of affects from the ideational material which generated them is the most striking thing which occurs to them during the formation of dreams. . . . A dream is in general poorer in affect than the psychical material from the manipulation of which it has proceeded [p. 467].

Freud thus distinguished between affects as determinants and affects as content, and there is no reason seventy years later to dispute this view. Subjective experience fails to suggest that dreams always begin with a distinctive change of affect, and confirms that dream affect is often inappropriately weak or strong relative to the concurrent imagery. The proposition that emotional arousal influences dream content is supported by evidence that viewing violent films before bedtime, which are presumably more arousing emotionally than nonviolent films, leads to more vivid, bizarre, and affective dreams (Foulkes & Rechtschaffen, 1964) and that college girls' dreams are least pleasant during the most depressed phase of the menstrual cycle (Swanson & Foulkes, 1968). Nevertheless these data are unable to shed light on the way in which particular dream segments are instigated.

Arousal During REM Periods. There is ample evidence that REM periods are characterized by elevated and irregular heart rate, elevated systolic blood pressure, faster and less regular respiration, penile erections, adrenal activity, and, in ulcer patients, elevated gastric secretion, functions often associated with affective arousal (Hartmann, 1967). For several reasons, however, this evidence provides no support for the proposed model. First, it has been shown that dreaming, even in the more restricted senses, occurs during NREM as well as REM periods (Pivik and Foulkes, 1968). REM periods have a statistically greater preponderance of the most distinctive dream-like mentation, to be sure, but there is as yet no evidence that physiological arousal is also associated with the more dreamlike NREM experiences. Second, REM periods are too long, too cyclical, and too regular for the mere association of arousal with REM periods to represent the instigation mechanism sketched above. Third, the present definition of dreaming encompasses all sleeping mentation, not just the more hallucinatory segments, and the model is intended to be similarly general. Therefore, until research on physiological arousal during dreaming can be refined to take account of the heterogeneity of dreams within sleep stages and the continuity among all levels of awareness, the evidence concerning differential arousal during REM periods is irrelevant for present purposes.

Arousal During Sleep Disturbances and Motor Activity. Apart from REM arousal, sleep is characterized by fluctuations in skin resistance and motor activity. Recent evidence indicates that galvanic skin responses (GSRs) occur during all stages of sleep but most prominently in deep sleep (Shapiro, Goodenough, Biederman, and Sleser, 1964). There is at present no evidence concerning a link between GSRs and shifts or accentuations of mentation, although such evidence could readily be obtained. There have, however, been studies of the relation between arousal and motor activity or sleep disturbances (Broughton, 1968; Rechtschaffen, Goodenough, and Shapiro, 1962).

Broughton (1968) has carefully documented the position that nightmares, night terror, sleepwalking, and bedwetting are disorders of arousal from deep sleep (EEG stages 3 and 4). Nearly all properly controlled episodes of these sleep disturbances occurred during moments of intense arousal from deep, slow-wave NREM sleep. The ideational precursors of such episodes are unknown. Broughton and other investigators seem to have restricted their inquiry into the ideational aspects to "dreams," defined as the more hallucinatory and vivid experiences, and seem not to have undertaken systematic investigations of the other forms of sleeping mentation that are more common in NREM sleep, where sleep disturbances originate.

Rechtschaffen, Goodenough, and Shapiro (1962) have reported that sleeptalking incidents during NREM periods were commonly accompanied by gross muscle tension artifacts, and that, in a few sleeptalking incidents monitored by psychogalvanometer, "Of 11 NREM incidents observed, 5 were accompanied by sudden decreases in skin resistance atypical for randomly selected intervals during sleep [p. 425]." Compared with NREM speech, REM speech seemed more affect-laden, and possibly more anxious.

Dement and Wolpert (1958a) have also reported that gross body movements in REM sleep are commonly followed by fragmented recall of dreams, whereas in the absence of movements recall is commonly relatively coherent. Taken together, these findings suggest that physiological arousal and body movements, in Dement and Wolpert's words, "mark the end of one dream sequence and the beginning of another [p. 545]."

There are, then, scattered bits of evidence for the presence of arousal at the onset of segments of several kinds of sleep activity—sleeptalking, sleepwalking, bedwetting, nightmares, and night terror. Of course, none of these phenomena are simply dreams or sleeping mentation. They lent themselves to investigation precisely because they provided atypical opportunities for behavioral observation. However, in light of the recognition that dreaming in the broadest sense occurs in all sleep stages—and may well be continuous during sleep—the possibility of important commonalities between these sleep disturbances and ordinary dreaming cannot be excluded. In any case, the data concerning them constitute the nearest empirical evidence relating physiological or affective arousal to the onset of dream segments.

Implications for the Instigation of Fantasies

A model has now been suggested to account for the phenomena of dream instigation, whereby dream sequences are elicited or directed serially by successive conditioned affective arousals. Borrowing Skinner's term, the sleeper is behaving in a respondent mode, the elements of his dream experience being elicited rather than emitted. Described in this fashion, the process of dream instigation bears some resemblance to Varendonck's (1921) description of daydream instigation, with the apparent difference that once a Varendonck daydream has been elicited it runs its course with considerable conformance to semantic and syntactic propriety, and often contains obvious and even prolonged elements of operant thought.

If one were then to describe a continuum extending from problem-solving operant thought through daydreams, hypnagogic ideation, and NREM mentation to REM dreams, it may be that one of the chief distinguishing differences is the prominence of emitted operant activity as against elicited respondent activity. To suggest such a dimension is, of course, to raise many questions. What, for instance, is meant by "prominence?" Is respondent activity amplified in the dreamier states or attenuated during goal-directed effort? What has the respondent-operant continuum to do with symbolism and communicability?

Meanwhile, insofar as fantasy and dreams share a continuum of baseline ideational activity, it seems reasonable to propose that some of the same instigators that appear to influence dreams also influence fantasy, though in a manner and extent that cannot, of course, be ascertained simply from evidence concerning dreams. Such an extension of dream theory to waking fantasy suggests the hypotheses that fantasies are potentiated by current concerns, are formed by schemata that conform on one or another level to the concerns that are contemporaneously active, and are steered by the capacity of the elements of ideation at one moment to cue off new affective responses laden with correspondingly new ideational elements.

SYMBOLIZATION IN DREAMS AND FANTASY

Previous sections have delved into such properties of dreams as their correlations and continuity with fantasy, their status as a baseline ideational process, and their instigators; but the property of dreams that seems to have attracted the attention of psychologists first, and the property that perhaps remains the focus of greatest interest to the layman and to the clinician, is their striking and often perplexing symbolism. It is the symbolism of dreams that has induced a number of theorists to take dreams as the point of departure of major theoretical statements (e.g., French, 1954; Freud, 1900; Jung, 1964) or as one of the major classes of data which their systems must accommodate (e.g., Piaget, 1945; Werner and Kaplan, 1963). Sciences often gain greatly by intensive examination of their strangest phenomena, and dream symbolism is certainly one of the strangest phenomena of psychology.

Basic Properties of Dream Symbols

Dreams as a Decipherable Code. The theoretical systems that have paid the greatest attention to dream symbolism have often been considered at great variance from one another, but amidst the sharp disagreements regarding concepts of mechanisms one may discern a surprising degree of underlying agreement on certain basic features of dream symbolism. All major theorists agree that dream symbols constitute a form of inner communication, the elements of which are a decipherable code. All seem agreed that the code consists for the most part of orderly transformations of cognitive responses that the individual acquired in the course of his conscious waking life. Although Freud and Jung have each at some points favored the existence of certain innate symbolic responses, contemporary Freudian and neo-Freudian analysts have stressed the acquired nature of symbols; and Jung has cautioned that by his "archetypes" he intended not symbols inherited in detail, but rather instinctive trends toward the use of certain classes of symbols, the particular form and details of which must be filled in by the dreamer with his acquired cognitive representations.

Dream Symbols as Response Elements. Several recent theorists have depicted the symbolic dream response as an instance in which the dreamer applies a pre-established cognitive response tendency to a particular dream situation. That is to say, individuals become accustomed in waking life to responding in certain ways to certain kinds of situations, and the mode of the response gives meaning to its object; in sleep, the individual continues to respond in accustomed ways, and generates a succession of symbols. In Piaget's language, the individual acquires a certain response "schema" for dealing with corresponding situations, and it is the successful application of such a schema that imbues the object of the response with meaning for the subject. In this sense, newspapers are a particular kind of holdable-and-readable, hammers are a particular kind of holdable-and-poundable, etc. When a child uses a telephone like a hammer (i.e., "assimilates" the telephone to the hammer schema), either because he doesn't know any better or because he is pretending, then the telephone holds for him the meaning, among others, of hammer. Children at play assimilate all sorts of objects into realistically inappropriate schemata, and the inappropriateness makes little difference to them as long as they can continue to "pretend." Dreamers also exercise schemata—cognitive, ideational schemata rather than motor ones—but their cognitive activity is even less constrained by external reality than is the child's at play, and, indeed, the dreamer is often completely unconscious of the external world. Thus Piaget (1945) concludes that "unconscious symbolic thought follows the same laws as thought in general, of which it is merely an extreme form, being an extension of symbolic play in the direction of pure assimilation [p. 212]."

Werner and Kaplan (1963) and French (1954) take remarkably similar positions. Werner, in fact, had long ago (1912) proposed the usefulness of the schema as a conceptual tool in thinking about human development. Like Piaget, Werner and Kaplan assert that objects and symbols are experienced as semantically similar when they evoke "inner-dynamic" similarities in what the individual does with them; and they point out that a schema comes to transcend the particular organs or limbs involved in responding to it. A paintbrush, for example, retains a common core of meaning whether held in the right hand or left, foot or mouth. These cognitive schemata are learned and stable. Just as play was seen in the previous chapter to consist of preestablished units, so Werner and Kaplan (1963) describe the response building blocks that underly the development of "depictive" responses in infancy—the forerunners of the symbols—as "differentiated as to elements and integrated into units that become progressively stabilized as stylized, recurrent, habitual sensory-motor forms [p. 86]."

The notion that dreams reflect stable cognitive structures—cognitive dispositions to respond in particular ways—is also consistent with French's (1954) use of the term "cognitive structure" as the ordering principle in dream symbolization. Schemata and cognitive structures become organized at different levels of complexity and abstractness, and a high-level schema may imbue rather diverse events with a common meaning of which the subject is unaware. For instance, "the mother's beating an iron bar in the manifest dream is equivalent in pattern to the fantasy of being beaten by the mother, which is one of its meanings, and also to the fantasy of being beaten by the father, which is another of its meanings; and the beating of the iron bar in the dream text also tends to satisfy the need to be 'beaten into shape' that would have been satisfied by his dreaming of being beaten [p. 8]." Thus the elicitation of a schema in dreaming incorporates an element of flexibility. In waking life, the particular response that an individual chooses to make is closely determined by reality factors. In dreams the choice of a particular symbol is determined otherwise, which brings us to another area of general agreement.

Plurisignificance and Condensation. One of the basic properties that Freud (1900) ascribed to dream symbols was condensation, the compressed representation in a brief symbolic episode of meanings that would take far more time and far more elaborate construction to represent in a more transparently communicable form. The dream symbol, in other words, is a powerful if somewhat cryptic metaphor, akin in this sense to the figures of poetry, art, and popular idiom. By virtue of being such a condensed communication, each dream symbol signifies many things and may be interpreted equally correctly at many levels.

No theorist has seriously challenged this basic view of the dream symbol, though the position has been translated into other theoretical terms, and theories vary widely in their explanation of it. Moreover, the ramifications of the view provide a means for understanding and interpreting the symbol.

If it is true that dream symbols are simply cognitive responses (schemata) exercised in the reality-vacuum of sleep, then one may say of both dream symbols and cognitive symbolic responses in general that each image or word is rich in perceptual and motoric associations, and that these associations vary in compass or abstractness. In addition to ordinary semantic associations, word symbols are also bound up with homonymic associations—puns, clang associates, rebus effects, etc. In Werner and Kaplan's (1963) term, symbols are "plurisignificant." The consequence of the plurisignificance in action is what Freud (1900) called "overdetermination" of images or behaviors, but overdetermination and plurisignificance go hand in hand. In waking states the symbol normally takes a particular manifest meaning from its context, and is often selected to fit into a goal-directed instrumental sequence. During sleep, by contrast, a simultaneous activation of several instigators (concerns, affects, associative chains, or whatever other instigatory process one may posit) induces that symbolic sequence which best incorporates meanings relevant to all of the instigators. Thus Freud's dream of perusing a botanical monograph that he dreamt he had written seems to have conformed in its various schematic meanings to the hoped-for completion of his real book on dreams, to his feelings about the already published accomplishments of his colleagues, to his pride—by now perhaps a somewhat defensive pride—over his publication concerning the coca plant, to his botanical failures during his youth, to the distractions of his book-related hobbies, and so on. Given that all of these elements were contemporaneously active during his night's sleep, they appear to have induced a symbol that conformed to each of them in some way.

The way the dream symbol conformed to the requirements of its probable instigators was not logical in the usual waking sense, nor was it fitted for ordinary instrumental activity. It was, rather, a plurisignificant coding of Freud's thoughts. In Hall's (1953a) words, "Dreaming is pictorialized thinking; the conceptual is made perceptual [p. 175]."

Freud (1900), of course, added to condensation the property of displacement, in that the dream symbols often seem to be only remotely associated with what the dream analyst decides is the really central, "latent" concern expressed in the dream. Thus affect and attention are "displaced" from a focus of interest to a somewhat tenuous representation of it. Piaget (1945) has pointed out that some degree of displacement is inherent in the process of condensation, since one cannot condense many referents into one symbol without displacing attention from the many referents to the single symbol. For Freud, the dreaming code is a defensive disguise, the result of "censorship" in the "dream-work." Adler (1931), Hall (1953a, b), Jung (1964), Piaget (1945), and others have each in his way rejected the doctrine that dream displacements are defensive efforts to distort and disguise, and each has marshalled powerful arguments against Freud's position. Nevertheless, there is general acceptance of displacement as a property of dreams, the obverse of condensation.

Such is the prevailing consensus regarding condensation. It must be added that very little direct experimental evidence exists to support the theory. However, there is indirect support, such as the discovery of semantic generalization (Feather, 1965); and an auspicious direct attack on the problem has been begun by Shevrin and Fritzler (1968) in synthesizing rebus effects. They found that after displaying tachistoscopic stimuli depicting both a pen and a knee at subliminal (.001 second) exposure durations, subjects produced significantly more "penny" responses in a subsequent free-association period than they did after .030 second exposures above threshold. The experiment thus establishes the existence of one mode of symbolization, and suggests means for further probes of symbol formation by experimental synthesization of symbol formation.

One further probe helps to shed light on the associational mechanisms of condensation and rebus effects, and suggests some of the factors that determine their prevalence in fantasy. Luria and Vinogradova (1959) instructed subjects to attend to particular key words and then studied subjects' orienting reactions to series of word stimuli. They found that in alert normal and mildly retarded subjects the orienting reactions generalized to words similar to the key word in meaning, but not to words similar only in sound. However, with mildly retarded subjects who were fatigued, orienting reactions generalized to words similar in sound, but not to words similar only in meaning. Thus it appears again that the conditions which lead to "dream-like" transformations of fantasy are not necessarily sleep as such, but a set of conditions normally present during sleep.

Symbols in Dreams and Fantasies

Dreams have always been regarded as more richly symbolic than waking fantasies, except perhaps in psychotic states. At one time, indeed, it may have made sense to consider waking and sleeping mentation as virtually qualitatively different in the role played by relatively unconstrained symbolism. In light of present evidence, however, it now appears equally clear that such a sharp differentiation is invalid. Dreams themselves vary sharply in symbolic value (Pivik and Foulkes, 1968), and rather dream-like productions are possible during awake periods, as in TAT stories told upon awakening from REM sleep (Fiss, Klein, and Bokert, 1966) and in associations following certain subliminal stimuli (Shevrin and Fritzler, 1968).

To consider the matter further, it is necessary to distinguish two separable but interrelated classes of symbolism. There is at present no factor analytic or other similar empirical basis for demonstrating that they indeed constitute two separate dimensions, although such evidence could in principle be obtained. Nevertheless, it seems reasonable to propose that symbols differ in at least two respects, morphological fusion and sequential fusion.

Morphological fusion refers to the creation of particular images that depart from constellations that the subject could have experienced while awake; for example, a rabbit with antlers, Freud's friend whom Freud experienced in the dream as Freud's yellow-bearded uncle (Freud, 1900), or neologism. Morphological fusion is one of the chief referents of ratings on the Dreamlike Fantasy Scale (Foulkes, Spear, and Symonds, 1966) for "bizarre" and "unusual" content, that characterizes the most "dreamlike" end of the rating continuum. Morphological fusion seems to occur very rarely in waking states except in the psychoses. However, it is possible that closer scrutiny of waking mentation would reveal a higher-than-expected incidence in normal waking states, particularly during certain creative efforts or in the little-understood state of "punchiness."

Sequential fusion refers to the weaving of otherwise plausible and coherent images into implausible or disjointed sequences; for instance, in Freud's dream of his son during the first world war, the scene shifted rapidly from Freud informing his wife of good news to their encountering his son in a store-room in sports clothes, and then to the son climbing upon a basket to reach a cupboard without speaking to his father. Despite the apparent disjunctiveness of the action, it was all experienced as a single connected dream. No individual image can be judged to be bizarre, but the sequential fusion of events nevertheless imparts a sense of the bizarre. Not all sequences need be so strikingly disjointed to fall in the category of what is intended by "sequential fusion;" for instance, a daydream like those reported by Singer (1966) of a boy's imagining his own baseball stardom and a long improbable series of his own personal triumphs on the professional baseball diamond would appear to be a weaker instance of sequential fusion. Viewed in this way, sequential fusion in one form or another occurs rather frequently in daydreams and hypnagogic states as well as in dreams.

If the present analysis is correct, then fantasies share with dreams the form of symbolic representation that is here dubbed sequential fusion, but fantasies generally do not share in the other form of symbolic representation, morphological fusion. It is possible to view the two kinds of fusion as two dimensions, one of which characterizes the difference between dreams and waking fantasy, and the other of which is independent of these states. On the other hand, it is also possible to view morphological and sequential fusion as different points on a single experiential dimension of fusion, a continuum in which the size of the segment that remains unfused becomes progressively smaller. Thus, in Varendonck's (1921) more business-like reveries there is never an instance of morphological fusion and rarely an instance of sequential fusion. In lighter fantasies and early hypnagogic states, sequential fusion is more frequent, drift is more rapid, and the persistence of a coherent segment is briefer. During REM sleep, the unfused portion of segments may vanish to the point at which even particular images are fused.

The notion of a single dimension of fusion can also be rendered as a dimension of progressive degeneration of integrated response sequences, a degeneration of the unknown mechanisms that maintain the elegant, skilled execution of overlearned motor and cognitive skills. This degeneration could hardly indicate deterioration of the associations themselves, but its existence would suggest that the organization of overlearned skill behavior requires either a level of activation or a kind of protective inhibitory process that is lost during REM periods and weakened in other nonoperant states. The plausibility of such an explanation is strengthened by the resemblance of morphological fusion to the kinds of morphological response errors made by individuals at the outset of skill learning, and the resemblance of sequential fusion to anticipatory goal responses and the kinds of errors attributable to negative transfer later in the skill-learning process.

These intriguing possibilities can be neither confirmed nor rejected in the absence of a program of experimental and multivariate analysis. At present, however, it can be said that a theoretical consensus exists concerning certain aspects of dream symbolism, that waking fantasy appears to contain some degree of symbolism, and that the prevailing concepts of how dream symbols are determined may provide clues to the determination of content in fantasy generally.

PROBLEM-SOLVING PROPERTIES OF DREAMS

Nearly every major dream theorist has proposed that in some sense dreams have positive functions in individuals' personal economies, that in some sense they help to solve problems; but an examination of the evidence for these assertions is particularly unsatisfying. First, few major theorists agree as to the function of dreams. Second, there seems not to be a single experimental investigation of their problem-solving properties. Third, the empirical evidence that is employed fails entirely to distinguish between dreams as reflections of concerns and dreams as resolutions of concerns. Fourth, all psychological illustrations of problem-solving functions depend on symbolic interpretations that proceed according to certain general interpretive principles, but are applied without regard for rigor and replicability. Nevertheless certain general comments may be attempted.

arguments

Recent investigators have shown experimentally that deprivation of REM sleep produces later compensatory increases in REM sleep and may be deleterious to integrated waking functioning (Dement, 1960). The finding was commonly accepted as proof that dreaming serves an empirically unspecified neuropsychological function, but the fact that dreaming occurs quite regularly outside of REM sleep (Pivik and Foulkes, 1968) and that the deprivation effect can be compensated by certain waking experiences (Cartwright, 1966; Cartwright and Monroe, 1968) greatly weakens the interpretation that dreams in themselves subserve the biological function. Furthermore, despite attempts to account for the findings in psychoanalytic terms, little evidence is available to indicate what psychological origin or function might be associated with REM sleep. Thus the REM-EEG studies have indeed discovered a new organismic need, but the discovery is not yet capable of illuminating the function of dreams.

Freud's (1900) original hypotheses ascribed several functions to dreams. At the most rudimentary level, dreams were regarded as a cushion for strong instinctual impulses, protecting the dreamer's sleep by diverting their energy. More psychologically, dreams provide partial instinctual gratification because, in the laws of the "primary process" operative during sleep, hallucination is gratifying. Dreams also were considered solutions of a kind—just as were daydreams and neurotic symptoms—in permitting a degree of gratification through a symbolic compromise with the defensive forces of the ego. In the course of reaching symbolic compromises, the dream-work synthesizes infantile wishes, contemporary day-residues, and defensive ego factors, and as a result the dream product is sometimes capable of yielding a resolution that suggests to the waking individual a possible real solution to his real problems, one that is to some degree gratifying and defensively acceptable. For Freud, however, these solutions are accidental "spin-offs," incidental benefits of a process hardly adapted as an agency of systematic problem-solving. French (1954) and Silberer (1951) have extended and emphasized this cognitive and adaptive aspect of dreaming, and suggested that it constitutes a legitimate function.

Foulkes (1966, 1967b) has applied REM-EEG techniques to bear on the question. From his analysis of adult dream series he concluded (1966) that the dream is "a purposive exploration of certain experiences and problems that occur in waking life [p. 70]." Although he also concluded (1966) that "Hallucinated wish fulfillments do appear in dream content, but they are not the key to its nature [p. 76]," a rich dream series he subsequently obtained from four prepubertal boys provided data fully consistent with Freudian or Eriksonian expectations, which, however, left his conclusions unchanged. There seems little question that by the undisciplined rules of orthodox psychoanalytic dream analysis the data could be made to support a wish-fulfillment theory as readily as Foulkes' impressionistic analyses have found support for a problem-solving interpretation. Despite the obvious productivity of his method and the insightfulness of his interpretations, the question remains unanswered. The resolution of this controversy will await neither polemics nor illustrations but rather the development of consensual, reliable methods for content-analyzing the dream protocols, so as either to allow the hypotheses to be discriminated empirically or to establish that the controversy is operationally intractable and thus scientifically meaningless.

Jung (1964) and Adler (1931) have approached dream function rather differently. Jung makes the problem-solving function of dreams central to his theory of mental functioning. Dreams are "the voice of nature," informing the individual of important neglected or unconscious facts and feelings about himself and his social relationships, and redressing the balance of defensive one-sidedness. Dreams thus potentially provide the dreamer with crucially important information which he needs in order to formulate his major personal decisions adaptively. For Adler, the pictorial aspects of dreams are far less important than their emotional content and the mood they set, which helps to reinforce decisions and to provide the pretext for actions which the individual was arriving at anyway in accordance with his consistent life-style.

Although these theories are speculative, they nevertheless bear in their broadest outlines a resemblance to the description of the problem-solving functions of play in the previous chapter. Dreams, like play and fantasy, are fractionated, unsystematic approaches that work over the dreamer's real concerns, and in the process sometimes yield solutions by generating new combinations of pre-established schemata.

CONCLUSIONS

1. The kinship of dreams with fantasy is reflected in a number of relationships which, taken together, seem persuasive although not conclusive. Individuals' dreams are thematically correlated with their drug-induced waking fantasies but not with their TAT stories. On the other hand, individuals' dream reports and TAT stories are related in their imaginativeness, length, and conceptual characteristics. Aside from these gross resemblances, there are a number of indications that dreams and fantasies are to some extent functionally interchangeable, the peculiar characteristics of dreams resulting from the differential effects of sleep stages upon a continuous ideational stream. Such a conclusion rests upon evidence that "dream deprivation," that is, REM sleep suppression, is reduced by permitting the substitution of waking dream descriptions and related fantasy-like ideation for the dream loss; that TAT stories told just after an awakening resemble structurally the kinds of dreams they replaced; that dream and waking mentation meet at their hypnagogic or hypnopompic boundaries without any obviously marked transition point, dream mentation bearing some of the characteristics of waking fantasy and supposedly characteristic dream phenomena occurring under a number of conditions during waking life.

2. The evidence that dreams and fantasy form a continuous ideational stream, together with suggestions in the previous chapter that fantasy forms a psychological baseline process during waking life, indicates that together dreams and fantasies form an unceasing psychological baseline whose particular characteristics are modulated by the state of physiological arousal that forms its context.

3. Dreams reflect those of the dreamer's current concerns—unconsummated behavior sequences and unrealized consequences—which can yield significant emotional arousal. Concern-related elements of one dream segment elicit affective responses that then govern the ideational flow during the next segment, and so on *seriatim*. Extending this model to fantasy leads to the hypotheses that fantasies are potentiated by current concerns, formed by schemata that correspond to the aroused affects, and steered by the capacity of dream elements at one moment to elicit new affective and ideational responses.

4. Dream symbolism constitutes a decipherable imaginal code. Symbols are formed so as to fit simultaneously the several ideational schemata that have become active at the same time. These schemata become active simultaneously because they are all responses to one particular dream element that touched on several of the dreamer's concerns. Since the constellation of concerns need not be coherent or homogeneous, nor the succession of affects logical, the resulting condensed symbolism seems inscrutable and distorted both morphologically and sequentially. Although waking fantasy seems rarely subject to morphological fusion, it frequently seems sequentially fused. In general, although the unfused elements of fantasy are more prominent than those of sleeping mentation, particularly in REM sleep, fantasy seems nevertheless subject to symbolic encoding, which may permit the extension to fantasy of what is known about dream symbolism.

5. The extent to which dreams exist as a problem-solving mechanism, or the extent to which they actually assist in the solution of problems, is still very much in doubt. However, like play, dreams appear to be fractionated, unsystematic reworkings of real concerns, and they are known sometimes to help reach solutions to difficult problems.

differences in imagery but led to little further analytic experimentation. Accordingly meaningful advances have depended largely on the progress of perceptual theory, verbal learning, and neuropsychology as they impinged on the subject of imagery.

Conclusion. The notion of imagery or idea has persisted in all major pre-behavioristic systems of philosophy and psychology. Its formal role has been to "explain" the operation of memory and sometimes thought and to provide units of analysis, however ambiguous, for the stream of conscious experience. To this date the relation of imagery to the memory mechanism is obscure, and the demonstration by Ach and his Würzburg colleagues that thought may be imageless, coming on the heels of the psychoanalytic revolution, seems to have convinced contemporary psychologists that directed thought cannot be analyzed completely into a succession of purely conscious components. This legitimate denial of the explanatory power of associated images does not, however, deny that conscious ideation exists as a phenomenon to be explained, that the flow of fantasy may be analyzed into components that may correspond experientially to imagery of some sort, or that the nature of those imaginal components is susceptible to experimental analysis. Such questions must be answered independently.

Since Aristotle, and especially since Augustine, ideation has been regarded as some sort of positive activity under the individual's control. Aristotle and Hobbes have stated with particular clarity their conviction that thought is of at least two different kinds, one with little voluntary direction, and the other voluntary and directed. This distinction, which has persisted, for instance, in sharp distinctions between primary and secondary process (Freud, 1900), autistic and directed thinking (Berlyne, 1965), or *A*-thinking and *R*-thinking (McKellar, 1957), will form an important part of the present analysis.

The long debate concerning the relative importance of innate and empirical contributions to ideational processes seems to have been channeled by the requirements of scientific explanation into productive investigative work. The development of general theories of evolution and of particular ethological theories has rendered the existence of innate structural determinants of ideation not only plausible but probable, and the argument now is essentially how specific is the innate determination, and in what manner do inborn determinants interact with the developmental history of the individual organism. Much more progress has been made in approaching this question concerning operant symbolic responses, motor skill learning, and conditioning than concerning fantasy as such.

The sections that follow, then, present an argument that images are responses, that fantasies are response sequences of certain kinds, and, therefore, that what we have learned about responses generally ought to be applicable to fantasy segments in particular.

FANTASY AS A RESPONSE SEQUENCE

The philosophic consensus that fantasy and other forms of thought are composed of ideas or sensory images, and that these are activities, suggests the easy course of asserting that fantasy is a succession of responses and then getting on with the business of exploring the implications of such an equivalence. Since, however, neither "activity" nor "response" mean in their application to ideation just what they mean in reference to motor events, the characterization of fantasy as a response sequence is a purely verbal exercise unless it can at least in principle be buttressed by evidence that fantasies possess the properties of other kinds of responses.

By response the psychologist ordinarily means an observable change in the organism's motor system or its central neural pathways. To put it another way, in viewing responses the psychologist is willing to accept what may broadly be called efferent events and their immediate observable consequences. If the definition of response were limited to overt motor events, then, strictly speaking, it would be impossible ever to study fantasy as a response system. At best, one could study verbal behavior that describes purportedly inner experience. Defining responses more broadly as efferent events, however, would render fantasy directly accessible to investigation as a response system; for efferent neural events can clearly be investigated, and it seems a safe prediction that one day fantasy-related neural events will be investigatable, despite the fact that present technology has permitted only a very slender start on the psychophysiological study of inner experience.

Thus in the broader sense of response as an efferent event, there is nothing illogical or absurd about proposing that fantasy may be investigated empirically and directly as a response system. Nevertheless, in the present state of knowledge and instrumentation, the argument in behalf of fantasy as a response sequence must necessarily be indirect and inconclusive, if perhaps nevertheless reasonably cogent. The strategy of the argument may take several forms. One can argue that since evidence is increasing that perceptual processes are at least partly efferent in nature, so probably are imaginal processes. One may try to show that just as known efferent events obey certain laws of acquisition, extinction, discrimination, integration, organization, and potentiation by drive states, so does fantasy or its imaginal components. One can cite evidence that neural elements of the central nervous system behave like known efferent processes at even a unit level, and argue that this enhances the likelihood that the neural substrate of fantasy is essentially efferent. Then, having bolstered the assertion that fantasy is efferent, one may proceed to draw out the implications for a theory of fantasy, bearing in mind that the derivation is conditional upon the validity of the argument.

Acting on this plan of procedure, then, we proceed to examine each element of the argument in somewhat greater detail. Because of the paucity of evidence that employs fantasy—or even verbal reports of fantasy—as a dependent variable after certain kinds of experimental treatments, the discussion that follows sometimes considers studies of imagery as well, on the assumption that the two kinds of events are sufficiently closely related to permit some interchangeability.

Efferent Properties of Imagery and Fantasy

The notion that an image is an efferent, response-like process may at first seem paradoxical, since the concept of image is so closely related to the concepts of sensation and perception, which have often been regarded as consummately afferent. The afferent quality of perception has occasionally been challenged, as in the turn-of-the-century controversy over the "motor theory of consciousness," and some recent investigations have returned to the question with new experimental analyses (Festinger, Ono, Burnham, and Bamber, 1967; Held, 1965; Held and Freedman, 1963). In addition, Tomkins (1962) has formulated an efferent approach to perception which places the construct of image at the center of the system. Nothing, Tomkins suggests, is perceived until the organism has acquired a central image corresponding to it. Indeed, "afferent sensory information is not directly transformed into a conscious report. What is consciously perceived is *imagery* which is created by the organism itself. . . . Before any sensory message becomes conscious it must be *matched by a centrally innervated feedback mechanism.* This is a central efferent process which attempts to duplicate the set of afferent messages at the central receiving station [p. 13]."

The virtue of such a construct—which is at this point purely hypothetical—is that it incorporates a mechanism for reducing the massive input of constantly varying information to a form within the organism's capacity to process. Since the matching of sensory and imaginal patterns need not be exact, the construct serves to explain stimulus generalization, the capacity to treat similar but nonidentical stimuli as functionally equivalent, and to underpin such concepts as Bruner's (1957) notion of perceptual category. It meets the objection often directed at associational theories of ideation, that the experienced image often bears only a rough, thematic correspondence to the original stimulus. Finally, the construct is able, if only loosely, to account for the basic facts of waking imagery, fantasy, and dreams, as well as the individual's capacity to distinguish them from reality, in terms of the activation of imaginal responses in the absence of confirmation by corresponding sensations.

Tomkins' theory is in some important respects incomplete. Except to characterize the matching process as a skill, he leaves unspecified the means by which images are acquired. The theory therefore is unable to suggest how it is possible for an individual to perceive consciously the details of such rapidly changing new events as a strange landscape seen from a moving train. Although Tomkins describes imagery as a critical part of retrieving memories from storage, by analogy with "outer" perception, it is unclear how the appropriate memory traces are potentiated or by what criteria successive images are selected in the flow of imaginal experience.

The theory leaves one other problem that also seems to have been overlooked by theorists in the areas of both memory and psycholinguistics despite the fact that it is inherent in the old associationist theories as well, as James (1890) pointed out (p. 584). The problem is best exemplified by the common instance of a "lost" memory or word, for which the individual is "racking his brain." What is theoretically problematic about this is that the afflicted individual "knows" the word he is searching for, is able to reject incorrect alternatives, and would pounce with recognition if the correct word were suggested to him, even though he is unable to produce it. Such a problem, of course, is likely to occur only during instrumental thought, not during revery, and the difference in probability of occurrence may well indicate something of the difference between instrumental thought and fantasy. However, it is also revealing of the nature of imagery. Since in Tomkins' system only imagery becomes conscious, the lost word must represent a defect not of memory but of the matching image; but, in that case, how does the individual recognize or formulate the experience of knowing a word which he cannot retrieve? Is there a third parallel system—parallel to memory and imagery—that has the properties of expectancy and that can edit out nonconforming imaginal sequences but is nevertheless incapable of eliciting conforming ones? Whatever the answer, the problem makes clear once again that thought cannot be confined to a succession of images, even though the imaginal sequence may be the facet of the total process that becomes available to conscious experience.

For present purposes, however, Tomkins' theory suggests the outlines by which a viable argument can be made in principle for the position that imaginal processes are efferent. Can the argument be supported by specific empirical evidence?

Perception as an Efferent Process. A perception is presumably something different from an image that is unrelated to concurrent sensation. Nevertheless, images are modality-specific—visual, gustatory, kinesthetic, etc. All theories of imagery assume that the imaginal mechanism includes at least portions of the perceptual mechanism (e.g., Evarts, 1962; West, 1962). Generally, imagery is described as overlapping the "downstream" part of the perceptual process, omitting the sense receptors, the peripheral nerves, and perhaps the more nearly peripheral of the central mechanisms. Penfield and Rasmussen (1950) report evocation of varied imagery by electrical stimulation of temporal lobe areas of the cortex, which are certainly well downstream of the more clearly afferent nerve tracts. If the perceptual mechanism could be shown to be efferent, that one could reasonably regard it much likelier, although of course not established, that imagery is efferent also.

The argument that perception—and, indeed, conscious experience in general—is efferent is an old one, championed at the turn of the century by Münsterburg and put most forcefully in the prebehaviorist tradition by Washburn (1916). Her theory in its most concise form is "that consciousness accompanies a certain ratio of excitation to inhibition in a motor discharge, and that if the amount of excitation either sinks below a certain minimum or rises above a certain maximum, consciousness is lessened [p. 25]." Thus the contraction of one's pupil with heightened illumination is unconscious, and so is a mother's admonition to a small child engrossed in "Mighty Mouse," if these can serve as instances in which inhibition of the appropriate response is, respectively, minimal and overwhelming.

Washburn broadened her category of movement to include hard-to-observe but truly motoric "tentative" movements, thus charting a theoretical tack which also characterized Watson's (1914) "implicit" response theory of thinking and the "peripheral" theory of mentation in general. Even in Washburn's day some evidence existed for such vestigial motor accompaniments of thought, but then and now the evidence was incapable of demonstrating that motor effector activity formed part of the mechanism of mentation rather than representing merely an "overflow" of the central process (Vinacke, 1952; Osgood, 1953). The issue is still undecided, and the persistent contrary indications (Humphrey, 1951) have led theory to retrench by postulating central mediating responses (e.g., Osgood, 1953) which are the vestiges of formerly overt responses, are not necessarily any longer motor in the strict sense, but may be described as efferent.

Washburn was not centrally concerned with perception, and she described perceptual processes as a mingling of sensory and response components in which efference seemed more nearly to characterize apperception —the connotations of a stimulus—than perception as such. In the behaviorist temper of the decades that followed, the problem of efference in perception was neglected empirically as a pseudoproblem but re-emerged as an intervening variable. Thus, for instance, Berlyne (1951), in an explication and elaboration of Hullian theory, treated perceptions as "stimulus-producing responses" on the grounds that they are subject to the influences of learning variables. Recently, however, the problem has been revived amid a flurry of experimental activity (Festinger, Ono, Burnham, and Bamber, 1967; Held, 1965; Held and Freedman, 1963; Merton, 1964; Taylor, 1962).

The new data proceed in several related directions. Merton (1964), for instance, reported methods for eliminating afferent information from thumb joints or muscles, with which he and his associates produced compelling evidence that a person's thumbs seem to him to point in the direction toward which he wills them to point, even if the experimenter has actually prevented them from moving there. Taylor (1962), Held and his associates (Held, 1965; Held and Freedman, 1963), and Festinger and his associates (Festinger, Ono, Burnham, and Bamber, 1967) explored the effects of interfering with normal feedback processes in vision and audition. Their most common procedures entail placing on their subjects eyepieces, spectacles, or contact lenses made of distorting prisms, whose effect is to displace the apparent location of stimulus objects, or to make straight lines appear curved. Under certain conditions, subjects adapt to these optical distortions; for example, lines that are objectively straight but form a curved image on the retina seem curved when the prisms are first used but come subjectively to appear more nearly straight or even entirely straight after the subject has used the prisms—under certain conditions.

The necessary conditions for adaptation require that the subject make active, voluntary responses that attempt to use relevant aspects of the distorted perceptions; for example, he may observe his hand through a distorting prism while moving it, or rapidly trace a distorted line, or walk while using distorting lenses to find his way. With appropriate feedback, subjects learn a new relationship between their movements and the visual or auditory sensations ("reafference") produced by the movements. Subjectively, the perceptions of these subjects come to conform with the movements which they are ready to make toward the stimulus world—that is, the subjective experience of stimuli depends on subjects' efferent activity in relation to them. Take, for example, a subject wearing distorting contact lenses which make straight lines project a curved image on the retina. If the subject is asked to track straight lines, he must make straight eye-movements, even though his retinal image and his initial perception of the line are curved. After a period of tracking, the distorted line will gradually become subjectively straight, to conform to the subject's efferent control of his eye movements. The key, however, is not the movement as such, but the subject's efferent control of the movement. Passive movement of the subject by the experimenter, for instance, has no effect.

The existence of these observations creates enormous difficulties for a purely afferent theory. They enable the conclusion at least that the reality of perception is far more complicated than the passive reception and coding of sensory afferent stimulation. The sense of position of one's limbs may well be predominantly a matter of where one thinks he has placed them. Orientation in space and the perception of contours seem to occur in an efferent framework within which afferent signals are interpreted. Whether all perceptual phenomena will some day turn out to require an efferent component is another question. It is at present difficult to construct an efferent theory of color discrimination or of the discrimination of musical patterns or odors.

These potential omissions from an efferent theory of perception would be highly significant for an efferent theory of imagery, since the experience of color imagery is a prominent part of the hallucinations reported by subjects during periods of sensory restriction, in which visual, auditory, and proprioceptive stimulation is sharply reduced; and both sounds and smells have been repeatedly reported in the hallucinations that accompany certain psychopathological states. However, it is unclear—and methodologically a possibly intractable problem—how closely these hallucinatory experiences indeed resemble the sensations attributed to them, and, of course, it is entirely possible that, however hard it may be to conceive, the central nervous system does possess the capacity for an efferent representation of colors, tones, and smells.

In any case, the imagery of normal waking life consists predominately of representatives of shapes, language, and motor activity, and, as we have seen, there is strong evidence to believe that the perceptions of contour and bodily position depend on a prominent efferent process. The suggestion that imagery and fantasy are at root efferent processes is thereby rendered at least highly plausible.

Learning Attributes of Imagery and Fantasy. If imagery is efferent, it should, like other responses, display the phenomena of learning, extinction, discrimination, potentiation by drive states, and the like. Although evidence on any one of these properties is very limited, their aggregate suggests that imagery is capable of respondent conditioning. Before reviewing the evidence, however, it is necessary to examine what it means to speak of imagery as conditioned or learned.

The traditional view has regarded imagery, which occurs as sensory-like experiences in the absence of the objects that the images represent, as some sort of internalization or imprinting of sensory impressions on the nervous system. This notion is at the root of conceptions from Democritus to Leuba (1940) and Ellson (1941) who speak of conditioned hallucinations and images as "conditioned sensations." However, this term implies that original sensory fields are stored in their entirety and elicited by appropriate cues. With the likely exception of certain eidetic images, the visual images of everyday experience are for most people far from veridical copies of what they represent. Rather, they consist of selected aspects of a total sensory experience, those aspects which were for some reason striking or important. Images may therefore seem much more nearly like retrieved *perceptions* than sensations, connoting by this the highly selective coding that appears to occur when a sensation is processed for purposes of response. Or, in the behaviorist's equivalent terms, the content of visual images reflects the cues to which the subject has learned to respond differentially or even the differential responses themselves—that is, the subject's learned discriminations.

This is not to deny that visual imagery may differ from other methods of storing or retrieving information. Sheehan (1966), for instance, has requested subjects to copy complex designs and later asked them to reproduce the designs in the absence of the original pictures. The reproductions contained generally fewer errors when subjects were requested to conjure up and describe mental images of the designs than when they were asked to recall the designs by other means. Furthermore, subjects who claimed generally vivid imagery were better able to recall designs of intermediate complexity, and their recall of unpatterned designs suffered less in relation to their recall of patterned designs than was the case with poor imagers (Sheehan, 1967).

Nevertheless, a number of the results in Sheehan's program of research indicate that his subjects' imagery depended on their ability to perform discriminations, rather than on some ability to store veridical reproductions for later inspection. Since Sheehan's instructions always requested subjects first to copy the design with blocks while the picture remained available, all subjects were required to perform some discriminations. Beyond this, however, Sheehan (1966) found that images of relatively simple designs were rated more vivid by subjects than images of more complex designs; that images of designs the elements of which had first been shown to the subject one by one were rated more vivid than images of designs that had not been so introduced; and that the images of good imagers gained vividness with increasingly many occasions of exposure. All of these variables would be expected to facilitate or retard the formation of discriminations.

Piaget and Inhelder (1962) have reported results from a quite different kind of research approach, but their data permit for our purposes a similar kind of conclusion. They reason that the quality of a child's imagery should determine his ability to imitate, copy, and extrapolate. The results of their extensive experimental observations indicate that, for example, since infants are unable to imitate movements in the model's absence until the age of about 14 months, the beginning of reproductive imagery cannot be demonstrated until an age that roughly corresponds to the onset of symbolic function; that deferred imitation of objects in motion is difficult prior to the age of five; that selecting the correct picture of a toppling object's trajectory from among a number of possibilities is difficult before the age of six, and so on. In the case of each task, the age at which success becomes likely corresponds to the age at which subjects normally acquire an intellectual grasp of the events to be copied or transformed. Thus, for Piaget and Inhelder, the intellectual "operations" come first, and the corresponding imagery follows as a consequence. In their view, then, imagery is a kind of interiorized imitation, a positive cognitive response, that is dependent on the subject's cognitive structure as are other responses.

Piaget and Inhelder of course recognize the limitations of their method. It can show them nothing directly of the imagery itself and is probably less direct than verbal self-report. Although they employ a variety of devices for discovering subjects' ability to respond, such as verbal description of solutions, drawings, and multiple-choice selection, their method cannot completely escape the criticism that the responses they use as indicators of imaginal development are confounded with sensorimotor and linguistic factors. Nevertheless, in aggregate and in view of the difficulty of employing alternative methods to test their hypotheses with small children, their demonstrations and argument seem reasonably cogent, to the effect that the formation of images presupposes the acquisition of relevant cognitive structures and discriminations. In this respect, then, images are distinctly response-like.

The reported existence of eidetic "photographic" imagery, which permits individuals to read the imaged pages of a book or perform calculations with an imaged slide-rule (McKellar, 1957), is sometimes taken as evidence that imagery is capable of veridical reproduction. From one experiment that applied strict criteria to distinguish eidetic from noneidetic imagery, the investigators (Haber and Haber, 1964) reported that although the eidetic 8% of their prepubertal subjects were able to produce prodigious detail in their imagery, the imagery of these subjects, tested immediately after exposure to stimuli, lasted at most a few minutes, and the subjects' memories of the stimulus pictures were no better than the memories of other subjects after the imagery had once faded. From this account, therefore, it seems more likely that these eidetic subjects were able somehow to protract the neural events consequent to sensory stimulation than that they were able to retrieve the original sensory field from storage. As for "eidetic" images produced from long-term memory, Barber (1959a) has pointed out that subjects' eidetic experiences are indistinguishable from hallucinations produced under hypnosis or drugs or "at will," and that in both the eidetic and the voluntary hallucinatory cases, "the S is not only able to call up an 'image' of an object or person and to banish it whenever he desires but he is also able to alter its form, color, duration, and location at will [p. 238]." In other words, the eidetic image is in these cases constructed, and it would therefore be surprising to find that it was unselective.

Nevertheless, despite much evidence that the imaginal process itself is response-like, a few rare individuals possess a quality of eidetic imagery so remarkable as to leave little doubt that sensory fields may be stored in the nervous system in exquisite detail. The detail in these images is, in fact, so fine as to overtax existing theories of response-based perception and discrimination. Stromeyer (1970) conducted an ingenious series of experiments with an "eidetiker." For instance he used sets of "computer-generated stereograms developed by Bela Julesz":

> Each stereogram consists of a pair of random-dot patterns. When a person looks at these patterns through a stereoscope, which presents one pattern to the right eye and the other pattern to the left eye, he sees a figure emerge in depth. When he looks at the random-dot patterns without the stereoscope, he can see neither figures nor depth [Stromeyer, 1970, p. 77].

Stromeyer let his eidetic subject look at a right-eye pattern with the right eye only and a left-eye pattern with the left eye only. Later, in the absence of the patterns, Stromeyer asked his subject to project eidetic images of both patterns and to superimpose one on the other. The result was virtually identical to what the subject could see through a stereoscope. The remarkable fact is that these random-dot patterns contained up to a million dots each! The subject could retain the million-dot patterns for up to four hours.

Clearly the memory base for such imagery permits virtually photographic levels of detail. Nevertheless, the formation of the images themselves was a matter of voluntary construction. Thus even in such rare cases of striking eidetic imagery, the imaginal process acts in some respects like a response process. What role, precisely, efferent elements play in eidetic imagery, and how the facts of eidetic imagery bear on other forms of imagery, it is too early to estimate.

In the case of ordinary memory images Bartlett (1932) has shown a progressive change over time in their details and sometimes in their fundamental Gestalts, according to definable laws of "leveling" and "sharpening." Thus it appears that images are unstable, gradually regressing onto their most distinguishing features, which in turn may become exaggerated. This gradual alteration in some ways resembles the alterations of conditioned responses, which become more specialized and refined over trials, depending on their eliciting cues and the contingencies of reinforcement. In this respect, then, images undergo changes similar to skeletal responses.

Another kind of complication in speaking of the learning attributes of images arises from the array of phenomena subsumed under the rubric "image." The present discussion has by implication eliminated from consideration imagery concurrent with sensation and visual after-images, since these cannot be considered components of fantasy, but their exclusion still leaves a number of other classes, prominently memory images, categorial images, imagination images, and hallucinations. Since all of these classes potentially carry implications for an efferent theory of imagery, it is important to examine them and to decide whether they may all be legitimately regarded as variants of a single, functionally unitary type of process.

Perky (1910) distinguished between memory images and categorial or "imagination" images following their delineation by Wundt (1902), who distinguished images of imagination as cases of "voluntary synthesis [p. 291]" in comparison with the more direct reproductions of memory. Such syntheses may be fanciful constructions or representations of synthetic "typical" instances of a category, and hence called "categorial" imagery. Thus one is likely to form different images of "my mother" and "mothers-in-general," and this is the distinction intended between memory and categorial imagery. To conceive of memory images as straightforward retrievals of sensory experience seems untenable in view of the objections raised above. It is manifestly impossible to treat categorial images so simply. Since one would have to introduce special notions of fusion, superimposition, summation, and so on to account for them, the process is much more easily described in terms of variations in responses than in terms of the "mental chemistry" of the early associationists. Thus both memory and categorial images are response-like.

The relationship of hallucinations to other imagery is also problematical. Phenomenologically, vivid hallucinations carry a conviction of their reality, as when one swats a nonexistent mosquito on an insect-ridden summer evening. However, hallucinations are difficult to distinguish from images methodologically and are often believed to form a continuum. The problem of defining hallucination objectively in experimental situations has dogged researchers in the areas of hypnosis (e.g., Barber, 1964a; Goldiamond and Malpass, 1961) and sensory deprivation (Suedfeld and Vernon,

1964; Zuckerman and Cohen, 1964).

The upshot of a great volume of work experimentally analyzing hypnotic phenomena is that while both hypnotized and unhypnotized subjects often report "seeing" or "hearing" nonexistent stimuli, they rarely report being convinced of the reality of these hallucinations, which by definition renders them ordinary images, and the subjects' reports are themselves easily influenced by their experimenters' mode of inquiry, expectations, and nonverbal reinforcements. A minority of subjects also report other effects that one might believe to be related to hallucinations if one assumed that hallucinations are essentially sensory, such as optical illusions and negative afterimages, but, again, experimental analyses have cast serious doubt on their reality. Thus, for instance, some of Barber's (1959b) subjects reported that they experienced appropriate negative afterimages following hallucinations of colored circles, and denied any theoretical knowledge concerning the afterimage phenomenon, but they described their afterimages in accordance with "textbook" expectations (e.g., green after red); whereas other subjects (Elsea, 1961, cited by Barber, 1964b) reported their afterimages following real stimuli in terms that often varied considerably from the textbook descriptions (e.g., aqua or blue after red). Thus not only is the validity of such reports cast in doubt, but again hallucinatory-like images act more like constructive, response-like phenomena than like sensory ones.

A reasonably objective criterion of an hallucination must, of course, incorporate evidence that the subject is behaving relative to the hallucinated content as he would if the content were real, under circumstances that render implausible any suspicion of dissembling on the part of the subject. Such conditions may be considered met in the case of certain psychotic episodes, most dreams, and some deliria. Whether the hallucinatory experience in these instances is qualitatively different from other imagery is still a moot question. It seems quite possible, however, that accepting the reality of an experience and the sensory or response-like properties of the experience must be regarded as separate questions involving separate mechanisms. Not only may a subject ascribe internal imagery either to mental processes or to external reality, but phenomenologically there are circumstances when even an objectively existent visual stimulus can be confused with ordinary visual imagery and its reality denied. Thus, in Perky's (1910) famous experiment, both experienced and inexperienced introspective "observers" believed that the experimental stimuli were mental images. The investigator projected several colored objects (a tomato, book, banana, orange, leaf, or lemon) at barely supraliminal intensities on a slowly moving screen in the absence of auditory stimulation, and instructed subjects to fixate a point on the screen until they had an image to report. There can be little doubt that subjects' confusion was quite genuine. More recently, Suedfeld and Vernon (1964) have provided evidence that "hallucinations" reported by subjects in a sensory deprivation experiment may in some cases have originated with light leaks and related objective stimuli.

The evidence, then, suggests that images aroused either by external stimuli or by internal processes may be interpreted as external stimuli, and both may under other conditions seem purely internal. In that case, it seems plausible that the quality of generating belief is imposed by given circumstances on images that are functionally and structurally quite similar. To be sure, images vary greatly in vividness from one person to another and from one occasion to another, for reasons that are still entirely obscure. One might venture to generalize that only faint stimuli and vivid images are susceptible to misidentification, as both Perky's and Ellson's work suggest, but nobody has seriously suggested that the continuum of phenomenological vividness really consists of discrete, qualitatively different categories of events. In view of these arguments, therefore, hallucinations may be considered members of the class of imagery.

To return now to the question of whether images display conditioning properties similar to those of overt responses, the experimental evidence appears limited in critical respects to investigations of conditioned hallucinations reported by the subject verbally (Leuba, 1940; Leuba and Dunlap, 1951) or by buttonpresses in a signal detection task (Ellson, 1941a, 1941b, 1942). Leuba (1940) himself perhaps best summarizes his engaging procedure:

During deep hypnosis two stimuli, such as the ringing of a bell and a pin prick on the hand, were applied simultaneously to the subject for some half dozen pairings; before being awakened from the hypnosis, the subject was told that he would remember nothing that had happened during the hypnosis (posthypnotic amnesia); a few minutes after being awakened, he was subjected to a succession of stimuli among which was one of the two stimuli originally applied, say the bell ringing; he was instructed to report at once if he experienced anything, visually, tactually, or in any other sense modality, besides the usual direct effects of those stimuli [p. 345].

It must be noted that the procedure succeeded in violating nearly all canons of formal experimental design and conditioning methodology. No controls were exercised to standardize or specify reasonably precisely the unconditioned stimuli (*US;* images of which served as the conditioned response [*CR*] in this experiment), the conditioned stimuli (*CS;* which were used to elicit the images of the *US*), the time interval between *CS* and *US*, the background stimuli, or the sample. The *US* used were pin and algesiometer pricks; taps on the hand; the sight of a stopwatch, scissors, slide of a Chinese pagoda, the subjects' glasses, and drawings of a fish, triangle or cube; the sound of a pencil tapping; and the smell of creosote. The CS used were the sounds of a bell, a cricket being snapped, the tapping or striking of an object against a wastebasket, can, or file cabinet, and a Victrola record; pokes in the subject's ribs, or rubbing his hands with a ruler; the subject's voluntary arm movements; and the sight of the experimenter's arm moving. The experimental room was sometimes a "semisound proof room" and sometimes the investigator's office. The subjects were 17 undergraduates who over a period of ten years chanced by at an opportune moment. Since all were hypnotized they undoubtedly represent a highly selected segment of the general population, but the lack of a sampling procedure forbids even the most conditional guess as to its identity. Hypnosis was used in order both to concentrate attention and to create amnesia for the conditioning procedure.

The purpose of examining the procedure in such detail is not to declare its results invalid in advance, nor, certainly, to punish its memory, but to express the irony that with its profoundly irregular procedure it obtained conditioning in 15 of the 17 subjects, and that the nature of both the hypothesis and the evidence is such as to render the results reasonably valid. The hypothesis, after all, was simply that the CS would by itself come to elicit from the subject a report of sensing a US, as, for instance, the sound of a bell which had previously been paired with the smell of creosote would later by itself lead a subject to report that he detected a smell somewhat like creosote. This the procedure clearly effected. The prime objection one might raise is that the use of hypnosis and the rather transparent purpose of the experiment leaves the procedure open to a charge of "experimenter bias"—that the subjects understood the experimenter's intent and consciously or unconsciously simulated a conditioning effect. As a result, one might continue, the apparent conditioning was attributable to some other mechanism than the conditioning process as it is commonly conceived. Leuba's only defense against this charge is that if his subjects were simulating, they must have been talented actors, since the protocols of the subjects' responses record a very high incidence of spontaneous surprise, bemusement, and shock.

Leuba's original experiment was subsequently extended (Leuba and Dunlap, 1951) with rather similar methods, the chief changes being that during acquisition subjects were asked verbally to identify the CS and US, and, during testing, instead of the experimenter presenting the CS to the subject, the experimenter asked the subject to imagine that the CS (or various neutral stimuli) had occurred. The results were consistent with the previous experiment. Three of the four subjects generally reported experiencing the appropriate *US* after exposure during testing to the *CS* alone.

The objections that were raised to Leuba's original experiment apply with additional force to this later one. However, independent evidence for the occurrence of conditioned hallucinations emerged from a series of experiments by Ellson (1941*a, b;* 1942) which employed a quite different experimental design. Here *US* was a tone with a gradual onset and decline, *CS* was a light or the passage of a fixed time interval, and the subjects were requested to report the occurrence of the tone by pressing a button. As many as 80% of the 40 subjects in Ellson's initial experimental group pressed the button one or more times in the absence of the tone during the test trials, as compared with 20% of 60 controls who had received no acquisition training and 53% of subjects who had received various intermediate amounts of training. Subsequent work (Ellson, 1942) using a temporal conditioning method produced a lower but still significant rate of hallucination and demonstrated that while the gradualness of the tone onset was indispensable to the production of hallucinations, subjects' knowledge of the nature of the experiment did not prevent a significant incidence of conditioned hallucination. Brogden (1950), who had earlier initiated the sensory preconditioning literature that is discussed below, employed a somewhat similar procedure except that tones were always presented at some intensity. He reported that subjects' auditory thresholds were reduced following a preconditioned light. In view of Ellson's findings the Brogden results might be attributed either to conditioned hallucinations or to some sort of summative, facilitatory effect. These experiments, then, appear to support the proposition that images can be acquired by a conditioning process roughly similar to that which characterizes the acquisition of overt conditioned responses.

Little is known concerning the extinction of imagery. Leuba did not systematically examine extinction but implied that it usually occurred fairly rapidly. Ellson (1941*b*) undertook a systematic investigation using the methods described above and found little tendency for extinction. The frequency of hallucinations, their latency, and their duration showed no discernible downward trend during 20 trials. Ellson suggested that perhaps the hallucination of the *US* is in these circumstances its own reinforcement. There were, to be sure, no competing responses, and subjects seem to attach some degree of conviction to their hallucinations.

The study of conditioned hallucinations is formally quite similar to the study of what is known as sensory preconditioning. In sensory preconditioning, as in the conditioning of hallucinations, two stimuli are presented in closely contiguous, overlapping pairs, the second stimulus of a pair (*US*), for instance a light, beginning shortly after the first stimulus (*CS*), for instance a tone. After a repeated presentation of the paired stimuli, the subject is trained to react to the *US* alone by making a measurable response, such as the rapid movement of his finger from an electric grid in order to avoid shock (finger withdrawal) or the involuntary palmar sweating response (galvanic skin response, or *GSR*) produced by mild electric shock. When this training is completed, using *US* alone as the stimulus, subjects are presented with exposure to the *CS* alone and, although the *CS* has never before been paired with the electric shock, the subjects frequently react to the *CS* with the response that they had learned to make to the *US* (Seidel, 1959). Subjects in this experimental treatment are compared with subjects in a variety of control treatments, one of which, called a pseudoconditioning or sensitization control, is commonly identical with the experimental treatment except that during the initial, sensory preconditioning stage of the experiment, the *CS* and *US* are presented not paired but singly, in random order. Since the experimental groups emit conditioned responses after the *CS* significantly more often than do the control groups, the presumption is that the sensory preconditioning procedure led to some linkage between the *CS* and *US*, such that, for instance, the tone had acquired some functional equivalence to the light and could elicit responses that had previously been conditioned only to the light.

Sensory preconditioning differs procedurally from the studies of conditioned hallucination in that subjects are never asked whether the *CS*, say the tone, leads them to experience the absent *US*, say the light. These studies therefore provide no direct evidence concerning the phenomenological question of whether their index of conditioning reflects or involves conditioned imagery. Also, the method of stimulus presentation makes no provision for gradual onset or offset of the *US*, which Ellson (1942) has shown to be necessary in certain circumstances to produce conditioned hallucinations. Nevertheless, the other formal similarities are sufficient to suggest that the procedures employed in sensory preconditioning might have some of the same imaginal effects as those used in conditioning of hallucinations.

To the extent that the two procedures may produce comparable psychological effects, the sensory preconditioning (*SPC*) literature provides some evidence relevant both to the question of extinction of conditioned imagery and to the broader question of its learning attributes. Seidel (1959) concluded from his intensive review that "in the most conservative sense, one might simply state that the SPC studies have given results different from those previously gotten in conditioning or those implied by any S-R mediational learning hypothesis [p. 71]." His chief reasons for this conclusion are that "the *GSR* in *SPC* does not seem to follow the normal extinction curve [p. 70]" and that "number of repetitions . . . , temporal order, and specific responses have little effect on the establishment of stimuli association in *SPC*" whereas "the importance of these factors in conditioning is well-established empirically [p. 70]." However, Seidel's objections to sensory preconditioning as a true conditioning phenomenon were premature and merit systematic reconsideration.

The argument concerning extinction has since been answered by Wickens and Cross (1963), who found regular extinction to occur in a sensory preconditioning study with human subjects.

The number of times stimulus pairs are repeated during conditioning is clearly a relevant variable in sensory preconditioning as in other conditioning experiments, since conditioning is absent with zero repetitions and present with several. It may be that conditioning occurs more rapidly in sensory preconditioning than in other kinds of conditioning. Hoffeld, Kendall, Thompson, and Brogden (1960) have reported maximum sensory preconditioning to occur after four trials of stimulus pairing, and a lower secondary peak after 200 trials. Since such maxima are unusual in the conditioning literature, they concluded that sensory preconditioning must be different from other conditioning. However, Wynne and Brogden (1962) obtained no better sensory preconditioning after four trials than Hoffeld, Thompson, and Brogden (1958) had obtained after 200, using similar methods. Their criterion of sensory preconditioning was generalization of avoidance behavior from one stimulus to the other. All of these studies were conducted with cats, and each level of the critical independent variable was represented typically by only four to six animals. Although these numbers are sometimes sufficient to attain statistically significant differences, they make for rather unreliable point estimations of particular expectable values. It thus still seems safe to conclude that sensory preconditioning occurs rapidly, reaching maximum association strength after perhaps as few as four trials; but evidence that the four-trial maximum may be a true maximum followed by a decline in strength of association between four and 200 trials, instead of an asymptotic value, must be considered still provisional and perhaps implausible.

Seidel's evidence for the existence of backward sensory preconditioning, in which the *US* precedes rather than follows the *CS,* seems based primarily on evidence by Silver and Meyer (1954) which the investigators themselves interpreted to indicate that backward conditioning is weak in sensory preconditioning as in other forms of conditioning. Newer evidence (Wynne and Brogden, 1962) indicates that in cats backward sensory preconditioning has no effect, nor does forward conditioning with excessively long intervals between the stimuli, as of 8 or 16 seconds. Wynne and Brogden found maximum sensory preconditioning with interstimulus intervals of 0 and 4 seconds. Since no half-second interval was presented, no comparison with the optimal interval for other types of conditioning is possible from these data. However, Wickens and Cross (1963), working with human subjects and four interstimulus intervals from 0 to .6 seconds, found the most effective interval to be .4, the next best .1, the third best zero, and the least effective .6 seconds, "an order similar to that found in interstimulus interval-curves in ordinary conditioning and in elements of a compound CS [p. 206]."

In arguing that sensory preconditioning occurs in the absence of apparent responses, Seidel's review assumes throughout that the stimuli used in sensory preconditioning elicit no responses apart from autonomic or instrumental reactions unrelated to the perceptual process. Since he observed no responses to the stimuli that he could consider unconditioned, he assumed that sensory conditioning must be an afferent, S-S integration process unlike S-R learning. His conclusion has since been buttressed by further results (Lovibond, 1959) that seem to rule out the possibility that human subjects' subvocal verbalizations mediate the connection between the preconditioned stimuli. However, evidence that perception is accompanied by consistent "orientating reflexes" (Voronin et. al., 1965) and, indeed, that the perceptual process may itself be partly efferent opens up other alternatives. Parks (1963) has shown that suppressing subjects' orienting reflexes by administration of chlorpromazine destroys the sensory preconditioning effect, which led him to conclude that the orienting reflex mediates the link between the stimuli. Since the orienting reflex seems, however, to be a component in all conditioning, the tenability of Parks' thesis as a mechanism specific to sensory preconditioning awaits further experimental analysis.

All in all, the history of experimentation on conditioned hallucinations and sensory preconditioning suggests that images, hallucinations, and their behavioral indications display properties of conditionability and extinguishability similar in important respects to these properties in other kinds of behavior, although certain of the parameters may differ in the direction of more rapid acquisition and, under certain circumstances, slower extinction. One may speculate that these parametric differences may be because the conditioning of imagery and sensory preconditioning can occur without the necessity of gross motor responses, and therefore generate less "reactive inhibition," to use Hull's term, because the effects of effort and fatigue are less pronounced. After all, the equivalent of what is called the conditioned response in S-R learning, a response derived from the unconditioned response elicited initially by the *US,* is in imaginal conditioning the imaginal representation of the *US* itself. In sum, however, the similarities seem more impressive than the differences.

Learned behaviors tend to show two other kinds of characteristics. One is discrimination, the tendency to make a response in appropriate external circumstances and to withhold it under inappropriate circumstances. The other is evocation of the response by relevant motivation. This very complex matter is considered in detail in Chapters 8 to 11. To summarize the conclusions reached there, people who are striving to obtain certain incentives are more likely than otherwise to engage in incentive-related fantasies.

Although it is difficult empirically to disentangle evidences of discrimination from effects of motivation because of the often amorphous qualities of the motivation concept, there appears to be some evidence that a subject's fantasy themes are governed to a degree by the appropriateness of external circumstances. Thus Clark (1952) found that immediately after male college students were shown female nude slides in a classroom setting they produced less manifest sexual imagery than after viewing nonsexual material, under task-oriented instructions to rate the nudes for esthetic appeal; and TAT stories written under the purported aegis of the Dean's Office in the presence of a highly attractive female experimenter contained less manifest sexual imagery than stories written in the presence of the male administrator. At a fraternity beer party, on the other hand, a pleasure-oriented viewing of nude slides produced greater manifest sexual imagery in immediately subsequent TAT stories than in TAT stories told without the prior showing of nudes. In a somewhat similar vein, Mussen and Scodel (1955) found that TAT stories following nude slides shown in a classroom contained less sexual imagery when the experimenter was a "formal, professional, and somewhat stern man in his sixties" than when he was a "young-looking, informal, permissive graduate student." Murray (1959) has reported reduced TAT sleep imagery in sleep-deprived subjects as compared with normally rested controls, in a setting which encouraged the deprived subjects to consider sleep an inappropriate activity. The basic finding was replicated by Nelson (Epstein, 1962), who found further that the suppression of sleep imagery below the level of imagery in control subjects required the expectation of further sleep deprivation.

Although these data have generally been ordered to various psychodynamic construct systems involving drives, reactive guilt, and defense mechanisms, the evidence for specifically psychodynamic interpretations is at best weak. Clark, for example, supposed that subjects' anxiety and guilt-arousal suppressed their sexual responding in the classroom, but that the anxiety and guilt were attenuated by the beer and atmosphere of the party setting. However, the hypothesis that the party setting fostered less guilt than the classroom setting, and therefore permitted a different TAT response pattern, was in fact contradicted in the TAT data themselves by the presence of at least as much sex-guilt imagery in the party stories as in the others. Moreover, the evidence produced by Murray (1959) and Nelson (Epstein, 1962), that TAT sleep themes are reduced when sleep-deprived subjects expect further deprivation and consider sleep inappropriate under the circumstances of the experiments, surely requires the postulation of a psychological process less dramatic than powerful drive-generated guilt feelings and repression. Accordingly it seems reasonable to accept the data at face value, as evidence of discrimination in the emission of certain themes in fantasy.

The evidence that exists, then, suggests that imaginal phenomena possess learning and conditioning attributes substantially similar to those of events that are generally accepted as efferent, response-like phenomena.

The Neuron as an Efferent Unit. To the evidence of efferent elements in perception and of the efferent-like learning attributes of imagery, it is interesting to add recent evidence that even single neurons are capable of activity and behavior modification akin to that of gross overt responses. O'Brien (1966) has produced evidence of single cell activity in classical sensory conditioning, and Fetz (1969) has shown operant conditioning of single neurons. Both investigators studied units of motor cortex, of cats and rhesus monkeys, respectively.

O'Brien's chief finding was the discovery of single neurons whose firing was a direct function of the conditioning process. As a light *CS* was repeatedly paired with a somesthetic *US,* the activity of certain neurons increased in response to light alone, significantly more than during sensitization control periods. These neurons also showed evidence of extinction and easier relearning. Thus the course of conditioning is reflected in the parallel activity of individual neurons.

Given the methods of classical conditioning, the neurons tapped by the microelectrode of course behaved as part of much larger-scale neural activity. The experiment by Fetz, by using an operant technique, was able to make food reinforcement contingent on the activity of a particular neuron. As a result, during acquisition periods the monkey subjects learned to increase the activity of the single target neuron in order to obtain food pellets, and, like O'Brien's subjects, demonstrated extinction of the single-neuron response in the absence of food reward. The investigation stopped short of determining what other neurons may have been involved in behavioral changes parallel to those of the target neuron. It seems likely that although reward was contingent on the activity of only a single neuron, an animal would be hard pressed to refine its response to only the single cell. More likely the activity changes included many other cells, and probably entire systems of response. Neural activity was "sometimes accompanied by specific, coordinated movements such as flection of the elbow or rotation of the wrist [p. 957]." When Fetz "reinforced activity of postcentral 'somatosensory' cortex cells, monkeys quickly learned to stimulate the appropriate receptive fields [p. 957]." Their generalized, gross self-stimulation certainly suggests that these experimental methods recruit complex behavioral and therefore neural systems. In these circumstances, it would be interesting to learn the results of reinforcing somatosensory units in deafferentated animals. Would the somatosensory units then display the same operant characteristics as motor cortex units?

Of course, no one can know what is the inner experience of a monkey as he learns to control the pellet dispenser, perhaps purely by internal activity without overt motor accompaniments. Is he engaging in repetitive ideation of some sort? Is he exercising operant control over more general mood states, like Kamiya's (1969) human subjects? The answers to such questions would shed far more definitive light on the basic question of this section: is ideation an efferent, response-like activity like overt responses? Meanwhile, it appears that neural subsystems are able to reflect precisely and perhaps to sustain the course of both classical and operant conditioning—to behave, in short, very much like overt responses. This evidence, though still scant and partial, is at least compatible with the conceptual treatment of internal ideational activity as essentially efferent.

Conclusion. This section began by sketching the outline of an argument. Ideational activity might be regarded as efferent; therefore as possessing the attributes of other response phenomena, if one could show that even perceptual activity is efferent, that ideational phenomena are modifiable according to the same laws of conditioning as are overt responses, and that the probable neural substrate of ideational activity is efferent. In looking at the evidence for each of these arguments in turn, it has become clear that there are no definitive proofs, and that, indeed, the evidence is quite incomplete on all counts; but insofar as evidence exists, it provides substantial support.

Are Images Necessary and Sufficient as Components of Fantasy?

Ideas and images, according to the Western philosophic tradition, are the components of the ideational stream, and in the Augustinian tradition they are all volitional activities. The previous section has attempted to support the argument that imaginal events are, indeed, responses, sharing with other, overt responses a common core of regularities. However, the argument has so far left unexamined the empirical evidence concerning the necessity and sufficiency of images as components of fantasy. The question has two facets. First, can fantasy occur without some kind of imagery occurring at all times? Second, is the process of fantasy exhaustively describable as a succession of images?

Can Fantasy Segments be Imageless? Similar questions regarding the necessity and sufficiency of images as components of directed thought have long occupied philosophers and psychologists, and became the focus of perhaps the most seminal controversy of prebehavioristic psychology. The history of the controversy and its implications for psychological theory are delineated in Humphrey's (1951) classical exposition, to which the present discussion is heavily indebted. The issues revolved about the clash between the "structuralist" position of Wundt and Titchener, that all consciousness is analyzable into sensations and feelings that are always present, versus the introspective results obtained during the first decade of this century in Külpe's laboratory at Würzburg by Mayer, Orth, Marbe, Messer, Watt, and Ach, whose trained subjects were able to detect neither sensory nor feeling properties during certain periods of consciousness, and who moreover were able to demonstrate that thought consists of and is directed by factors that may remain unconscious. The controversy is often referred to as concerning the existence of "imageless thought."

The notion of imageless thought subsumes two issues which are best kept separate. First, there is the finding of Mayer, Orth, and Marbe that some conscious experiences cannot readily be classified under any of the rubrics commonly employed to describe imaginal thought. To denote these experiences they devised the term *Bewusstseinslage,* or state of awareness. Bühler suggested that thought was basically nonimaginal and that sensory imagery served sometimes only to illustrate, as it were, the objects of thought. Titchener's rejoinder on the basis of his subjects' introspections was that the apparently nonimaginal states really consist of faint kinesthetic imagery. When the two contentions proved irreconcilable by means of introspective data, their stalemate provided perhaps the single most potent justification for abandoning the introspective method in psychology. In retrospect, it seems that the highly trained introspective "observers" had been pushed to form discriminations beyond their capacity. In view of their failure, and in view of the absence of more recent relevant data, it would be foolhardy indeed to form a judgment concerning the pervasive presence or total absence of all imagery during any period. Titchener's observers in good conscience reported imagery of some kind at all times; the Würzburg observers did not. Recent research on sleeping mentation by Pivik and Foulkes (1968), Orlinsky (1962), and others have provided evidence of some mental content during most of the awakenings of subjects during NREM as well as REM sleep, but their findings hardly demonstrate the presence of imagery at all awakenings. Thus *most* periods of consciousness can be confidently asserted to contain imagery, but the possibility of imageless periods cannot be ruled out, and the issue must be regarded as still unresolved.

The second issue subsumed under the imageless thought controversy concerns the existence of unconscious determinants of the direction and mechanisms of thought. The Würzburgers Watt and Ach clearly won this argument, and in the process contributed significantly to the psychology of directed thought. They were able to demonstrate that the assignment (*Aufgabe*) with which the experimenter instructed his subject determined the class of the responses which the subject subsequently emitted; and yet the operation of the experimenter-instilled "determining tendency" or "set" was wholly unconscious during the process of responding. During the same period of history, the first decade of this century, the psychoanalysts were similarly driving home their argument for the operation of unconscious determinants of conscious ideation. Thus began the development of "dynamic" theories, dynamic because they represented behavioral outcomes as the resultants of often unconscious psychological "forces." The dynamic formulations, especially those of Freud, Lewin, Hull, and Neal Miller, which dominated personality theory and much of behavior theory during the 1940's and 1950's, either denied or ignored the necessity that the determinants and mechanisms of directed thought must in all cases be conscious.

There is no reason at this point to deny the validity of their accumulated analytic and empirical evidence, which clearly indicates that there is more to the process of directed thought than is identifiable in conscious imagery. Much of the early work to establish this generalization was performed with word associations, from which one might be tempted to conclude that the generalization is valid as well for projective test fantasy and even for free fantasy, but no direct, systematic introspective evidence is available to support such an extension.

The broader matters concerning what determines the sequencing of fantasy segments and concerning the motivational and stimulus determinants of fantasy are discussed in later chapters. What is relevant here is that the existence of imagery as an aspect of all conscious experience—imagery of one kind or another, including efferent components—cannot be ruled out.

Are Fantasy Segments Imagery Only? Even if one accepts the ill-supported conclusion that fantasy is at all times imaginal, there are compelling reasons to suppose that the imaginal aspect of fantasy is part of a larger process; that is, not only is the flow of fantasy segments determined in part by unconscious factors, but the fantasy segments are themselves response complexes whose ramifications extend beyond the purely imaginal responses which register most clearly in awareness. There are three lines of evidence to support such a position.

First, since thought and fantasy are directed by factors independent of imaginal content, the process of fantasy must embrace response elements in addition to imagery.

A second consideration, less decisive to be sure, derives from the pre-

generalize to words similar in meaning more often than to words similar only in sound. Although the mechanism of such semantic generalization is still a matter for conjecture, its existence appears reasonably well established (Feather, 1965). Luria and Vinogradova, however, found that certain conditions alter the direction of generalization. Mentally retarded adolescents tended to generalize less to words similar in meaning and more to words similar in sound, in proportion to their degree of retardation. Furthermore, mildly retarded subjects tended to shift from semantic to phonetic generalization as a function of fatigue. In studies employing lowered light-sensitivity thresholds as a conditioned response, Schwarz (1948, 1949) found a shift from semantic to phonetic generalization after administration of chloral hydrate, which is commonly used as a hypnotic and sedative.

It would be interesting to investigate the incidence of paradigmatic, syntagmatic, and clang associates in word association as a function of these same variables of fatigue and chloral hydrate. If, as was suggested previously, paradigmatic associates represent operant responses learned as appropriate to gain social reinforcement, decline in paradigmatic responses with increasing fatigue may represent a special case of the decline of feedback-using, complex response sequences.

To speculate further, these relationships may be relevant to the study of psychotic thought. Mintz (1948) and Singer (1966) noted certain structural similarities between sleepy speech and schizophrenic speech. The examples of disordered speech in hypnagogic and hypnopompic states cited by Mintz were uttered in full conviction that they constituted sensible, communicative statements. They apparently felt like well-executed skilled acts. The phenomenon of rapid drift in frame of reference that often characterizes REM dreams and seems to crop up after prolonged sleep loss also occurs frequently in schizophrenic thought. Chapman, Chapman, and Miller (1964) have further noted that directed schizophrenic thought tends to assign to words their dominant, most practiced meaning even when the context of the word suggests the appropriateness of a weaker meaning. Again, this phenomenon appears explicable as the product of disintegrated feedback-using mechanisms in the stream of thought and a breakdown in the requisite complexity of segmental organization.

The rise of clang, syntagmatic, and semantically dominant association pathways in states of fatigue or sleep, together with disintegration in the time-extended complexity of segments, offers an explanation of symbolism in dreams and allied states. Examples of dream symbolism are rife with symbolic puns (Freud, 1900), such as the summation of a phonetic association and a syntagmatic one in the dream ascribed to Alexander of Macedon (Freud, 1900, p. 99). During a long siege of Tyre (Tyros), Alexander dreamed of a satyr (satyros) dancing on his shield. "Sa Tyros" may be translated "Tyre is thine." The rebus association thus symbolized can then be seen as the resultant of associative regularities that seem more characteristic of sleep-like states than of normally alert waking states.

The way in which dream symbols may be induced receives attention in Chapter 3. There emphasis is placed on a continuum of response degeneration that in its more extreme forms was called "morphological fusion" and in its milder forms, "sequential fusion." Morphological fusion refers to such contaminated images as rabbits with antlers. Sequential fusion refers to the stringing together into one story line of episodes unlikely to follow each other in reality-oriented accounts. In light of the preceding analysis of response integration, the phenomenon of fusion can now be reconsidered.

First, fusion of whatever kind retains important indications of organization. The rabbit *with* antlers is a coherent, organized dream percept, however improbable, and its representation is configurational rather than disjunctive, as it might be if it were a rabbit *and* a pair of antlers. To the dreamer, the image is a natural, automatic event which he experiences during the dream with an undisturbed sense of conviction. Similarly, improbable sequences unfold automatically and carry a sense of conviction, even though sometimes accompanied by a feeling of eeriness. Individual episodes are configurational in that the characters and actions are represented as to some extent related to one another.

Second, what is striking about fused sequences is that the time span of integration is reduced below that necessary to carry out effective instrumental actions. Thus the longer term organization that characterizes instrumental cognitive activity comes apart at its more vulnerable points. Presumably one contributing factor to degeneration is the irrelevance of evaluative feedback to noninstrumental activity. If, as seems likely, instrumental cognitive activity entails expending metabolic energy at a slightly higher rate, and requires a higher level of activation, the time-binding operation inherent in the use of feedback to guide instrumental behavior is a biologically expensive process, likely to be abandoned when unneeded. In that case, the span of integrative organization is likely to collapse upon smaller segments, ultimately being reduced in REM sleep to organization at the level of very brief imaginal sequences, or to the level of the phrase or clause, thus producing a high degree of sequential fusion. The substantial abandonment of feedback comparisons with reality-based expectancies further permits the occurrence of morphological fusion.

Implications of Response Integration for Fantasy

Segments as Integrated Response Sequences. In the formulation of response integration presented here, an integrated response sequence is hard to delimit according to stable and clearcut criteria. As long as an organized behavior sequence unfolds relatively smoothly and automatically, requiring little conscious attention to its motor aspects and only routine processing of stimulus feedback, it may be said to display the properties of integration. Its integration is neither a rigid chaining of motor elements nor an irreversible linking of responses. There are thus no standard lengths of integrated sequences, and the length of even a particular type of integrated sequence seems to depend on physiological factors operating during a particular occasion. This is not to say, however, that response integration cannot be measured. Indeed, its defining attributes as employed here readily suggest measuring operations.

Among other variables, there should be some relationship between segmentation in fantasy and response integration. Changes in the thematic content of ideation of the kind used to delimit "main routines" constitute junctures or interruptions in the organizational unity of a sequence. Subsubroutines only a single sentence long would seem to constitute a level of integration relatively impervious to degeneration during waking periods. If segments indeed bear a close relationship to response integration in fantasy, analysis of the segmental structure of ideation may provide clues to the span of the plans, meaning-complexes, motor programs, or subselves that govern the integrated sequences that follow. The present theoretical formulation suggests the desirability of exploring empirically the intercorrelations between the characteristics of behavior that define response integration and the segmental organization revealed by a coding analysis of shifts in verbal content.

The Maintenance of Concurrent Activities. One of the hallmarks of overlearned, repetitive motor skills is the person's ability to undertake a second activity concurrently with the first. Walking, to cite an extreme example, is compatible with a wide range of motor and verbal activities, provided they make no conflicting demands on one's legs. Far more artificial skills can, however, be overlearned by subjects under laboratory conditions and carried on at the same time as reading, arithmetic calculations, and the like.

To be sure, there are important limitations on the maintenance of concurrent activities. They must employ different behavioral systems to avoid mutual interference. Thus, two activities which require simultaneous but different perceptual scanning are impossible, unless they may alternate. Since humans can entertain only a single train of thought at a time, two integrated ideational response sequences are incompatible. Apart from such obvious sources of incompatibility, there are others that Peterson (1969) has attributed to demands on attention. Tasks requiring little attention are presumed to be most easily compatible with other, concurrent activities.

Peterson avoids defining attention and indeed makes little use of the theory of attention, but he derives a tripartite classification of activities, in ascending order of demand on attention: emissive, reproductive, and problem-solving. Emissive activities involve the unfolding of a routine plan, such as the recitation of an overlearned passage from memory, and presumably require little feedback apart from some degree of self-monitoring. Reproductive activities require the subject to match a stream of stimuli with a corresponding stream of responses, as in reading aloud. Reproductive activities clearly require both closely focused perceptual activity and feedback monitoring to assure accuracy. Problem-solving activities, in Peterson's terminology, require some sort of "relatively complex transformation of the input [p. 377]," as in arithmetic calculations.

There are, of course, other ways of conceptualizing the parameters that govern the ease with which activities can be undertaken concurrently. Bahrick, Noble, and Fitts (1954) produced evidence that unpredictability of stimulus elements in a perceptual-motor task makes it incompatible with a concurrent arithmetic task. Schmidt (1968) pointed out that one theory of response automatization emphasizes that during acquisition there is a gradual elimination of conscious cues; consequently, if a task prevents the anticipation of cues it defeats the automatization of response.

To summarize, activities interfere with other, concurrent activities insofar as they require perceptual vigilance, utilization of feedback, and cognitive transformational operations. Fantasy requires no perceptual vigilance, no directed use of feedback, and no directed cognitive transformations. It is in Peterson's terms essentially a nondirected emissive activity, requiring little attention. Since it makes use of imaginal and verbal responses, it seems to be suppressed or displaced by directed thought and is therefore also incompatible with motor activity which requires transformational thought. Fantasy may nevertheless occur concurrently with a wide range of other relatively integrated motor activities and those kinds of perceptual activities not requiring close attention.

Antrobus, Singer, and Greenberg (1966) found that subjects in an auditory discrimination task, having to identify a brief tone as of a high or low frequency, reported engaging in moderately frequent task-irrelevant ideation. Three variables affected the fantasy rate. It declined if the stimuli succeeded one another at briefer intervals; if the subject was instructed to report whether a tone was of the same or different frequency than the previous one, instead of merely reporting high or low; and in accordance with increases in money incentives for accurate detections. Similar evidence regarding fantasy during motor activity is unavailable.

Effortlessness. Ordinarily, integrated response sequences emerge without the sense of groping and self-urging that often characterize less well-learned activity. The sense of autonomy of the behavior, once initiated, is characteristic. There are, of course, circumstances of fatigue and physical strain which make even an integrated sequence effortful. Fantasy, however, is physically rather undemanding. Ideation continues through all stages of sleep.

Singer (1966) has undertaken an introspective study of intrusions of extraneous thought and effortfulness in varying kinds of ideation. He set himself the task of thinking certain kinds of thought and subsequently recorded descriptions. He found that " [t]he frequency of intrusive thoughts was by far the greatest for complex, impersonal, and planful or theoretical material. Reminiscing proved to be the easiest task and produced fewest interruptions and the least feeling of strain [p. 41]." He also reported a strong "tendency for visual imagery to become increasingly prominent and to replace either more abstract thought or interior verbalizations. The visual material consisted chiefly of memories, but occasionally there were fairly elaborate fantasies of scenes that *might* take place . . . [p. 41]." Complex impersonal material was interrupted more often than simple impersonal material, whereas with personal material complexity made no difference. "By far the simplest line of thought to maintain was a memory sequence. Once initiated, a memory sequence seemed to run its course almost automatically, while theoretical thought or future planning constantly called for volitional effort. The contrast between planful thought and remembering was somewhat analogous to that of the early phases of learning a motor skill compared with the relative ease, integration, and quasi-automatic flow of motor activity once the skill has been acquired [p. 42]."

Feedback and Fantasy. Fantasy seems to meet the criteria for response integration suggested above at the outset of the present major section. Fantasy can be segmented, it proceeds smoothly and rapidly, it shows evidence of organization within segments, major portions of it seem to unfold in a fairly automatic, largely unplanned fashion, it is often easily forgotten, and it requires little concentrated effort. In the nature of fantasy, it probably cannot occur concurrently with other ideational activity, at least consciously, but it can occur concurrently with integrated motor activity, probably including the motor execution of preplanned sentences.

If a fantasy segment, then, may be regarded as a type of integrated response sequence, where is it located in the three-space generated by the three dimensions of response integration suggested earlier: complexity, number of potential elements per schematic component, and dependence on feedback? With respect to complexity, the question can probably not be answered without detailed empirical comparisons between the depth of fantasy segments and segments of directed thought. Probably, fantasy segments vary widely in complexity, and their complexity may well be related to arousal variables.

With respect to the number of potential elements per component, the answer is essentially a probabilistic one, a measure of the certainty of particular responses, in the information-theoretic sense. Thus, in a given operant situation, the number of appropriate responses may be severely limited by the requirements of the situation, and the probability of one or a few responses may then be high and the probability of many others correspondingly low. In fantasy, ideational elements are presumably less constrained by such instrumental considerations, but whether the probabilities of response are therefore more evenly distributed remains an empirical question. Quite possibly the stimulus, subself, current-concerns, and antecedent-ideation determinants of fantasy effectively constrain fantasy elements as much as or more than instrumental situations. Again, the answer requires empirical analysis.

The use of feedback probably differs in fantasy in comparison with nonfantasy activities. In operant activity, feedback is employed continuously and prospectively as a means for assessing progress toward completion of a plan or schema. Here the criterion for progress is some desired effect on external reality or the probable usefulness of an emerging set of problem solutions. Fantasy by definition cannot be guided by such criteria. Something other than feedback of this kind must therefore govern the transition from one fantasy segment to another. However, the unfolding of a particular fantasy segment may still be governed by feedback of another kind. If each segment is organized through an antecedent meaning-complex that controls the unfolding of the segment, there is probably some process for comparing the fidelity of the unfolding segment against the content of the meaning-complex. This kind of feedback is different from the previous kind in that it involves no comparisons with events or processes besides the segment and its meaning-complex.

Even though fantasy segments make no use of the kinds of feedback that are essential to the direction of operant sequences, a particular fantasy segment or even a dream segment may contain integrated operant activity. I recall vividly a dream, which may have been partly hypnopompic, in which I engaged in reasonably skilled debate with a policeman concerning the constitutionality of a traffic ticket. I was able to cite an obvious flaw in his procedure and perform correctly a simple arithmetic calculation in my defense. The debate seemed in retrospect entirely competent, even though the recalled onset of the dream segment was typically dream-like, much of the dream was symbolic, fused, and hallucinatory, and the dream was terminated not by the attainment or abandonment of the goal but by my spontaneous, late-morning awakening. My affect during the dream was as I explicitly labeled it in the dream: Kafkaesque. Yet, although the activity in the segment was goal-oriented, the place of the segment in the longer sequence and the nature of the segments that followed it were quite unlike what they would have been had the segment been part of an actual goal-striving sequence. It therefore seems reasonable to regard it as a segment of integrated operant activity which was in this context functionally non-operant, in the crucial sense that it was not emitted but elicited by prior dream events and that both its termination and the determination of the next segment seemed under the control not of goal-attainment or goal-abandonment but of its interruption by a wholly new kind of segment, unrelated to the first.

If fantasy segments and states are sequenced in accordance with feedback principles other than those which govern goal-striving, it is necessary to reconsider the role feedback may play. In fantasy, it seems likely that the unfolding nature of one segment influences the variables that contribute to the determination of the next segment. Thus, instead of the Test-Operate-Test-Exit model of feedback use that Miller, Galanter, and Pribram (1960) ascribe to operant activity, fantasy probably follows a pattern of Elicit-Unfold-Elicit-Unfold-Exit. Presumably, then, fantasy occurs within a sleeve of sensory determination as does nonfantasy activity, but the source of feedback is different. In operant motor activity, the sensory flow is a function of the operation of motor behavior upon physical objects—the body, the visual field, etc.—and the significance of feedback for further behavior depends on comparison of the raw sensory feedback with the planned goal of the activity. Fantasy leaves the environment unchanged, and by definition there is manifestly no planned goal against which to evaluate its progress. Under these circumstances, the operation of feedback is quite different. Fantasy responses produce changes in stimulation only insofar as their content instigates further ideational content or arouses affect. If segments are governed internally by plans, meaning-complexes, motor programs, or subselves, then the effects of fantasy on feedback occur at the end of segments, rather than continuously as in the case of continuously monitored, directed verbal or other motor activity. Fantasy may thus be considered directed by feedback but not corrected by it. Fantasy is ballistic, not guided. It is hurled forward at each juncture by the new processes cued off by its preceding content, but its aim is blind and unintentional.

Viewed in this way, the issue raised by the role of feedback in fantasy is really the question of how fantasy segments are sequenced. That, then, is the question addressed by the next chapter.

CHAPTER 7

Modes of Sequencing

The sequencing of fantasy segments can be viewed from two different time perspectives. One class of determinants of content exerts a relatively long-term influence, encompassing periods of hours, days, or longer. This class of potentiating factors has taken the conceptual form of "unconscious wish," "need," "drive," "motive," and, in the formulation of Chapter 3, "current concern." It is of great importance, and is considered extensively in Chapters 8 to 11. However, precisely because a determinant in this class exerts a relatively persistent influence, it is incapable of accounting for moment-to-moment shifts in thematic content. It is necessary, conse-quently, to consider a set of shorter-term determinants of sequencing, de-terminants that operate upon the transition from one particular segment of fantasy to the next.

It should be apparent from the preceding chapters that the concept of segment refers to a relative unit of organization rather than an absolute unit. Segmentation refers to changes in content. Content may change in basic thematic respects, leading to the designation of "main routine shift," or there may be a change in the focus of a continuing thema, which has been labeled "subroutine shift" (Chapter 4). The term "segment" is ap-plied to both main and subroutines indiscriminately. There is too little em-pirical information concerning segmentation to warrant sharp distinctions between these different levels of organization except for purposes of con-tent analysis.

Chapter 6 concerned itself with the composition and organization of segments. Implicitly, "segment" there referred to the smallest discernible unit of content, which might be a simple, fleeting main routine or a sub-subroutine in a complex main routine. One of the fundamental problems of psychology is to understand the causes of shifts from one such segment to another, to understand the dynamics of moment-to-moment behavioral change or, to state it another way, the laws which govern the sequencing of segments in behavior. The sequencing of segments in fantasy forms the subject of the present chapter.

182

TWO MODES OF SEQUENCING

The history of thought about thought is marked by a persistent dualism. Repeatedly, theorists argue for the necessity to consider two quite distinct classes or principles of thought, even though in nature the two are liberally intermixed. Aristotle distinguished between "passive reason," which corresponds roughly to undirected thought, and "active reason," which corresponds roughly to directed thought (Windelband, 1901). Hobbes (1651) put the case clearly:

This Trayne of Thoughts, or Mentall Discourse, is of two sorts. The first is *Unguided, without Designe,* and inconstant . . . : In which case the thoughts are said to wander, and seem impertinent one to another, as in a Dream. . . . And yet in this wild ranging of the mind, a man may ofttimes perceive the way of it, and the dependence of one thought upon another. . . . The second is more constant; as being regulated by some desire, and designe . . . [p. 9]."

The developers of associationist psychology sometimes attempted, as we have seen, to divest themselves of the duality and of the separate sets of principles that such a duality would entail. The modern consensus is that they failed, and the limitations of single-process associationism produced a variety of opposing positions and a number of interesting attempts at synthesis. Thus Brown (1836) posited a principle of "simple suggestion," embodying classically associationist principles, to account for fantasy-like thought, and a principle of "relative suggestion," an inherent tendency of mind to recognize relationships among objects, to account for the phenomena of reasoning. J. S. Mill resorted to the concept of a "mental chemistry" which transforms closely associated ideation. Bain found it necessary to buttress an otherwise "pure" associationsim with principles of discrimination and "similarity" and some relational assumptions, and Lewes introduced an organizational principle of "grouping" (Warren, 1921).

Perhaps the most extensive treatment of the two modes of thought, and certainly the one to exert the greatest influence on modern psychological conceptions, is Freud's *Interpretation of Dreams* (1900) and his subsequent papers on the distinction between the primary process and the secondary process in ideation. The primary process is characterized as fundamentally wish-fulfilling through the medium of ideation itself, as in the hallucination of an object of desire unfettered by logic or reality, organizing its associative networks around drives (e.g., table-food) rather than around reality-based concepts (e.g., table-chair), and capable of the hallmarks of the dream: condensation, displacement, and symbolism. It operates, in Freud's term, in accordance with the "pleasure principle" of fulfillment now. The secondary process, in contrast, is characterized as fulfillment-seeking but also reality-respecting, unwilling to mistake symbolic for real satisfaction, governed by the rules of logic and the laws of the real world, and organizing its associative networks around reality-based concepts. It operates "in the service" of the pleasure principle but according to the discipline of the reality principle of obtaining what is possible and safe according to optimal tactics for coping with the real world, deferring gratification when necessary. In Freud's theoretical framework, dreams are virtually pure representatives of primary process and daydreams are predominantly so, while directed thought predominantly represents secondary process. However, since Freud's notions of the primary process originated with his attempt to account for the structure of dreams, it seems best to regard the theory as a systematization of his observations of dreams, which has proved useful when extended also to the analysis of fantasy, psychopathological symptoms, and creative writing.

Freud's form of the dualistic distinction has spawned parallel concepts by other writers. Thus Varendonck (1921) distinguished between undirected "foreconscious" or "affective" thought and "conscious," directed thought. McKellar (1957) preferred to speak of "A-thinking" and "R-thinking." Berlyne (1965) reflected the consensus in much of contemporary general psychology when he sharply separated "autistic" from "directed" thought and, characteristically, spent little time on the former. Hilgard (1962) remained true to the Freudian dichotomy while suggesting the labels "impulsive" and "realistic" thinking. Despite the variation in labels and applications, Freud's (1900, 1911) "two principles of mental functioning" have remained substantially unchallenged as a descriptive classification and have been widely accepted by students of dreams, fantasy, and literary composition. They thus deserve close scrutiny for their contribution to the understanding of sequencing.

Implications of Primary and Secondary Process for Sequencing

The accounts of primary process appear substantially to agree on certain features that set it off from secondary process. Some, like the processes underlying the determination of symbolism, are of great interest but have little relevance for the sequencing of fantasy segments. Other features, however, seem directly relevant, and permit certain deductions which may be considered under five headings.

1. Unconcern with Impact on the Environment. The dominant characteristic of Freud's concept of primary process is the immediacy with which wishes yield gratification. Since immediate real gratification through reflexive action is generally unattainable, the wishes in primary process generally yield rather unsatisfactory results from an "objective," secondary-process standpoint—massive affect, hallucinations, and other, more diluted substitutes such as fantasies. In primary process, whatever gratification occurs in the absence of fortuitous real satisfaction is achieved by accommodation of the "psychic apparatus," of intracranial function, rather than by instrumental action of the organism on the world about. The lack of real impact on the environment is not simply a matter of ineffectiveness. Primary process as such entails rather an utter unconcern with effective action. It operates along dimensions on which the question of effectiveness is unrepresented, meaningless.

2. Unconcern with External Feedback. Since impact on the environment is an alien concern in primary process, so is the reception of external feedback. In addition, the notion of primary process entails a freedom of ideational events from any responsibility for directed thinking. The immediate ideational representation of a wish or an immediate, massive discharge of affect leaves no room for evaluation of results.

3. Absence of Feedback-Using Correction. Since primary processes are unconcerned with feedback, they are unable to use it in order to modulate the flow of ideation. Primary processes have wishes but no external goals and no mechanism with which to assess feedback and employ it to guide future behavior. Thus primary processes as such incorporate no correction of behavior, no editing of thoughts, no comparison of ideation with norms of logic.

4. Drive Organization of Associations. Rapaport's (1951b) formulation employs the term "drive organization of memories" to characterize the associative network which early in the life of the individual is built up around the experience of frustration of a particular drive. He regarded ideas within an associative network to be readily interchangeable and organized without regard to the relationships among the represented objects in reality. Thus, in primary process, aroused "drives" lead to a stream of drive-related ideation, but not to instrumentally usable ideation. It seems worth noting that Rapaport, like most writers in the field, seemed not to define "idea." One may infer that the term refers to an extensive range of phenomena, from an hallucination of a breast to a complex ideational sequence having a unitary theme.

5. Involuntary Quality. Primary process ideation has been variously described as peremptory (Klein, 1967), involuntary or effortless (Rapaport, 1951a, 1951b), and sometimes ego-alien. These terms refer to a property of the relationship one feels to one's own dreams, hallucinations, and, to a degree, his fantasies. Such experiences are not "willed." They are not planned. Rather, they occur. There is no sense of setting them in motion, no feeling of effort as in pursuing the solution to a baffling problem.

The involuntary or effortless quality of fantasy has been noted also by other investigators. James (1890) wrote: "If we could say in English 'it thinks,' as we say 'it rains' or 'it blows,' we should be stating the fact most simply and with the minimum of assumption [pp. 224–225]."

Singer (1966) introspectively investigated some correlates of the type of content in revery, expecially the susceptibility of a type to intrusions of unrelated thought. Singer's fantasy experiences were "tasks" deliberately initiated according to an experimental design. He found that "The frequency of intrusive thoughts was by far the greatest for complex, impersonal, and planful or theoretical material. Reminiscing proved to be the easiest task and produced fewest interruptions and the least feeling of strain [p. 41]." He also reported a strong "tendency for visual imagery to become increasingly prominent and to replace either more abstract thought or interior verbalizations. The visual material consisted chiefly of memories, but occasionally there were fairly elaborate fantasies of scenes that *might* take place . . . [p. 41]." Complex, impersonal material was interrupted more often than simple, impersonal material, whereas with personal material complexity made no difference. Singer further wrote: "By far the simplest line of thought to maintain was a memory sequence. Once initiated, a memory sequence seemed to run its course almost automatically, while theoretical thought or future planning constantly called for volitional effort. The contrast between planful thought and remembering was somewhat analogous to that of the early phases of learning a motor skill compared with the relative ease, integration, and quasi-automatic flow of motor activity once the skill has been acquired [p. 42]."

In extreme cases, for instance in paranoia, the individual disowns experiences dominated by primary process and attributes them to external causes, but even in ordinary instances individuals have little feeling of ego-control over their onset. The prescription to "stop worrying" is justifiably considered useless. At best, individuals can reduce the incidence or duration of undirected waking thought by engaging in incompatible activity which may crowd out the unwanted ideation. The only psychological control over the incidence of noxious dreams is to avoid sleep.

The implications of the Freudian theory of primary process, then, are that segments of activity which operate predominantly in accordance with primary process are sequenced without regard to feedback and without instrumental intent, are elicited and directed by active drives, and occur without conscious volition or effort. This characterization of primary process is, of course, to be taken in contrast to the properties of activity that predominantly reflects secondary process, which is instrumental, closely governed by feedback concerning its effectiveness in attaining a goal, and subjectively volitional and effortful, as in directed problem-solving thought.

Unfortunately these interesting propositions, which have such cogency as straightforward deductions from psychoanalytic theory and seem so consonant with most writers' introspections, stand almost without reference to hard experimental evidence. The imperviousness of dreams to feedback seems evident enough, in view of the general unreceptiveness of sleepers to any kind of stimulus input and in view of the fact that dreams have so little access to the dreamer's motor apparatus. Indeed, during REM sleep muscles are extraordinarily relaxed, which seems a very adaptive state of affairs when one considers the wildness of the ideational processes usually then in progress. The responsiveness of instrumental activity to feedback seems equally plain. No one, however, has attempted to investigate the responsiveness of free fantasy to experimentally introduced feedback. Such investigations of course would face the imposing methodological hurdle of gaining access to the continuous content of free fantasy, a problem that has been approached in our Morris laboratory but not yet completely solved (Chapter 4). McClelland and Winter (1969) have shown that the content of successive TAT stories can be shaped over a period of days or weeks by "training," but such efforts probably entail variables other than those intended here, since subjects' TAT stories in such settings constitute deliberate instrumental acts involving probably considerable conscious effort. We are left, then, with such introspective reports as Varendonck's (1921) that the stream of fantasy "cannot correct the mistakes which it makes in its progress, because the phenomenon which we call reflection is denied to it [p. 137]."

There have been many experimental studies of motivational effects on perception and projective fantasy, and a few of drive effects on dreams. These are reviewed at length in Chapters 9–11 and are therefore omitted here. In sum, to anticipate the next chapter, certain kinds of experimentally induced drive states may affect both dreams and projective fantasy, but the effects are often weak and their representation in fantasy is probably not direct and immediate. Nevertheless it seems likely from both experimental and clinical data that aroused constellations of affects, cognitive responses, etc., do consciously mark the onset of fantasy segments. The role of affects specifically in the sequencing of fantasy is considered later.

Everyone seems to agree that dreams seem effortless and nonvolitional and that fantasies often seem so, but no one, apparently, has produced systematic data to support the assertion. The question of degrees of effortfulness of various mental activities seems to have some similarities to psycho-physical studies of the amount of effort required to lift various kinds of weights. Everyone knows that a feather feels lighter than an anchor, but systematic data have nevertheless been very useful. A study designed like a psychophysical scaling project might be able to produce evidence on the degree of effortfulness of a variety of behaviors, thereby systematizing what are now just casual judgments and providing a more rigorous basis for the classification of behaviors.

Respondent and Operant Modes of Sequencing

In the absence of better data it nevertheless seems possible to deduce further some theoretical links between the foregoing essentially psychoan-alytic description of two modes of thought and another conceptual system, that of B. F. Skinner (1935, 1953). Skinner distinguishes between two classes of behavior defined in terms of the operations performed to pro-duce them. One class of operations consists of presenting the subject with an unconditioned stimulus (US) which is followed by a particular kind of response with sufficient consistency to permit the inference that the US "elicits" it. When the US is paired with a conditioned stimulus (CS) often enough in the Pavlovian classical conditioning paradigm, the CS comes to elicit a similar response. Skinner calls this process "respondent condition-ing" and the behavior "respondent behavior." A second class of operations induces a drive state by physiological deprivation, for instance of food or water, or by a noxious stimulus, such as electric shock. The subject is en-abled to discover an act which provides relief from the drive state, such as by delivery of food or water or by diminution of shock. On future occa-sions, especially in the presence of similar drive states, subjects will come routinely to "emit" the instrumental act necessary to obtain relief. Skinner calls this experimental procedure "operant conditioning" and the behavior "operant behavior."

The first parallel between the Freudian dichotomy of primary and sec-ondary process and the Skinnerian dichotomy of respondent and operant behavior resides in the distinction between "elicited" and "emitted" behav-ior. Emission entails making a response in reaction to inner events, pre-sumably as part of a goal-directed plan of action. In the typical Skinnerian experiment, emitted responses come to be the learned, guided behavior which was previously established and maintained by the experimenter's manipulation of the feedback inherent in reward or relief. In these respects emitted behavior conforms to the distinguishing properties of secondary process. Elicited behavior, on the other hand, is generally reflexive and in-voluntary. The two classes of behavior can be distinguished from each other experimentally even when they take the same gross form of response; for instance, voluntary eyeblinks differ in a number of subtle respects from involuntary conditioned eyeblinks (Grant, 1964, 1968). Respondent behavior resembles primary process activity in its largely nonvolitional nature.

The comparison between respondent and operant behavior in imperviousness to feedback is more complicated. In respondent conditioning experiments the US is by definition never neutral, and in successful conditioning the CS loses its neutrality for the subject. The stimuli in respondent conditioning therefore often possess motivating properties and may come to serve also as discriminative stimuli for the emission of operant behavior. In successive trials the unconditioned response (UR) to the US is gradually transformed as it becomes a conditioned response (CR) to the CS, often by attaining a greater economy of effort. Such modification suggests the utilization of some kind of feedback, but the role of feedback is far less prominent than in operant acts and is, as we shall see, differently utilized.

Furthermore, the occurrence of URs and CRs depends in most instances on USs which are in some way drive-relevant. Thus respondent behavior for the most part conforms to the distinguishing properties of primary process with respect to volition, importance of feedback, and elicitation by drive-related arousal.

A second parallel resides in the role of goals or reinforcements. Emitted behaviors and secondary-process activities are controlled by reinforcement delivered at their termination. Such sequences may be more or less flexible and capable of alternative circuitous approaches directed at a particular goal (Murray, 1937). Indeed, learned operant "responses" are often defined in terms of their final effects on the environment, such as depressing a bar, rather than in terms of the topography of the response sequence itself, such as moving one's hand through a certain path at a certain rate of speed (Staddon, 1967). Elicited behaviors and primary-process manifestations, in contrast, are controlled by the events that precede their onset and are likely to be defined in terms of the topography of the response sequence. Although respondent acts may often be adaptive, it makes little sense to describe the initial moments of leg flexion as an *attempt* to escape shock, or the startle reflex as an *attempt* to mobilize oneself for action. They are reactive, not proactive. In the case of traumatic avoidance learning, as in learning to avoid an electric shock to one's foot by moving the foot right after a CS warning signal, respondent responses prove far more difficult to train and, once trained, are very unstable in comparison to operant responses (Turner and Solomon, 1962). Whereas successful avoidance of shock reinforces operant avoidance responses, it extinguishes respondents. Respondent acts display little evidence of flexibility or other indications of goal-orientedness. In each of these respects, respondent acts seem to occur in relation to antecedent stimuli rather than to a prospective goal, much like the activities that display the properties of primary process.

A third parallel, less clearly definable, resides in the properties of effort. We have seen that dreams and fantasies are widely believed to seem phenomenologically effortless. Their effortlessness derives from something other than simply their ideational status, since directed, problem-solving thought can seem to require considerable "mental" effort. Respondent acts seem to share this property of effortlessness. Some typical respondent events are glandular, such as salivation, or autonomic, such as pupillary reflexes, but even such vigorous skeletal-muscle respondent acts as the knee-jerk following patellar stimulation or the startle response are strikingly nonvolitional and entail no sense of effort during their execution.

For all the apparent agreement concerning the relative effortfulness of various activities, however, there are remarkably few data and little conceptual analysis. Many writers fail to distinguish the sense of effort from the sense of volition. Ach (1910), however, in the course of a painstaking introspective analysis of volition, observed a clearcut distinction between the two. Volitional acts seemed to him possible without any sense of effort. Effortfulness, rather, seemed to depend on the degree of "concentration of the will" required to overcome obstacles in the path of attaining a goal after the initial act of volition had already occurred. Accepting for the moment that the sense of effort is introspectively distinct from the sense of volition, there still remain varying possible introspective interpretations of "effortfulness," such as exertion in mobilizing one's energies, concentration that requires one recurrently to inhibit extraneous ideas, the feeling of being drained by a task, and probably others. Since these distinctions have generally not been explored systematically and have been ignored in apparently all modern treatments of the topic, statements that some activities are less effortful than others are at least highly imprecise.

Not only have introspective analyses of the sense of effort fallen far short of incisive analysis, but studies of its behavioral correlates are nearly nonexistent, although Aveling (1931) reported that the sense of effort is accompanied by changes in skin resistance. Behavioral studies have focused on the effects of physical effort and fatigue, which are, of course, different matters.

Perhaps operant behavior feels less effortful when a subject can organize his activity around external stimuli instead of having to regulate and maintain a sequence of acts by purely internal means. Düker's (1931) subjects seemed agreed that performing a long series of successive tasks such

FANTASY, OPENNESS TO EXPERIENCE, AND CREATIVE THINKING

Men have long regarded creative acts as somehow different from ordinary instrumental acts and have expressed their awe by such terms as "inspired," meaning literally breathed into, presumably by supernatural agency. Creative ideas sometimes seem to "come to one" as a bolt out of the blue, and yet they cannot readily be coaxed or forced by effort of will. In the present formulation, creative ideas arise as respondent processes that are primed by current concerns. They therefore feel involuntary and must be accepted hospitably and recognized as salient if they are to benefit the problem solver.

Previous sections have suggested two chief means by which respondent processes may influence the course of an operant sequence. First, a person may intentionally suspend operant activity in order to permit respondent processes to work over a problem that is the focus of a current concern and perhaps to produce useful new insights. Sometimes a concern persists for very long periods—weeks, months, perhaps even years—and in these cases natural lapses in operant activity may also provide occasions for such respondent working-through. Second, respondent activity, attenuated but not obliterated, may inject continuous information into the problem-solver's operant processes, thereby helping to shape, warn, remind, and alert. These two means by which respondent processes can contribute to problem-solving entail somewhat different constellations of behavior and may even constitute different kinds of creativity. The first is often associated with retrospective accounts of major creative achievements in the arts and sciences. The second resembles a type of thinking skill that Barron has regarded as "originality" and Guilford as "divergent thinking."

Respondent Processes and the Creative Act

Just what constitutes a creative act is much disputed, but Koestler (1964) has suggested a fundamental property which pervades many categories of literary, artistic, and scientific creation and of humor. The moment of creative insight occurs when an individual recognizes that an element embedded in one frame of reference belongs also to another frame of reference, its double membership thus revealing a relationship that can solve a problem. Consider, for instance, an ape with a tree in his cage and food placed outside the bars beyond his reach. He knows how to use sticks to bring the food within his reach, but he has no sticks available. The problem is unsolvable until he recognizes that a branch of a tree belongs also to the class of stick-tools. The insight enables him to tear off the branch and use it as a tool to obtain the food. This act of insight Koestler calls a "bisociative act."

The crucial prerequisite for a bisociative act is that two hitherto separate frames of reference intersect in a common element. As long as an individual follows well-learned sequences of operant activity, he will continue to regard the two frames of reference as separate and the solution will therefore elude him. He needs something more, which takes the form, in the language of this book, of a respondent response potentiated by a current concern. The process can be described as follows.

One must assume first an individual in a state of current concern over solving a problem whose solution is momentarily blocked. His concern increases the likelihood that he will respond affectively to concern-related stimuli and, by generalization, to other stimuli or ideas that bear some resemblance to them. His affective responses to any of these stimuli carry with them respondent segments whose content very likely includes elements of operant sequences relevant to the goal of the concern. If the individual now encounters a stimulus or idea that resembles a concern-related stimulus in some nonobvious respect, his respondent response will bring it into close juxtaposition with concern-related operant activity. He responds to the new stimulus as if it belonged to the problem-solving frame of reference, thereby fusing the two and producing the bisociative act.

The process can be illustrated by Koestler's account of Archimedes' famous discovery:

Hiero, tyrant of Syracuse and protector of Archimedes, had been given a beautiful crown, allegedly of pure gold, but he suspected that it was adulterated with silver. He asked Archimedes's opinion. Archimedes knew, of course, the specific weight of gold—that is to say, its weight per volume unit. If he could measure the volume of the crown he would know immediately whether it was pure gold or not; but how on earth is one to determine the volume of a complicated ornament with all its filigree work? Ah, if only he could melt it down and measure the liquid gold by the pint, or hammer it into a brick of honest rectangular shape, or . . . and so on. . . .

One day, while getting into his bath, Archimedes watched absent-mindedly the familiar sight of the water-level rising from one smudge on the basin to the next as a result of the immersion of his body, and it occurred to him in a flash that the volume of water displaced was equal to the volume of the immersed parts of his own body—which therefore could simply be measured by the pint. He had melted his body down, as it were, without harming it, and he could do the same with the crown [pp. 105–106].

Archimedes was strongly motivated to solve the problem. He was preoccupied by ways to measure volume, which included liquifying the metal. Although he had not previously regarded bathwater in the same frame of reference despite its liquidity, the rising water in this instance had enough in common with volume-measuring situations to elicit powerful orienting and volume-measuring responses, because his strong concern had sensitized him to stimuli that even remotely resembled concern-related elements and had potentiated concern-related responses to them. The repertory of volume-measuring responses already included the measurement of liquids and were thus easily able to accommodate the measurement of bathwater. The bisociative act had occurred, leaving Archimedes with only the need to work out the details. The probable mechanism for the bisociative act was thus the concern-produced responsiveness of a respondent segment to a subtly relevant external stimulus.

The Conditions of Creativity

A problem-solver can benefit from his respondent channel only in the presence of certain conditions. First, he must possess the response capabilities implied in the respondent-sequence formulation of fantasy. Presumably everyone is subject to respondent activity as an ideational baseline process, but the particular forms which such sequences assume differ from individual to individual in accordance with the segmental forms (subselves, ideational schemata, etc.) which the person has had an opportunity to integrate. Thus some persons' respondent sequences may be more complex, sophisticated, or articulate than those of others. Not everyone, for instance, is equally given to organized daydreams, and, indeed, one finds wide individual variations and group differences in the patterns of daydreaming (Singer, 1966). Creativity is correlated with other measures of intelligence; high intelligence is no guarantor of creativity but high creativity is rarely achievable without a reasonable degree of other intellectual capacity (Guilford, 1967). Indeed, there is some evidence that skills in divergent thinking, or the "heuristics" of creative problem-solving, to borrow a term (Newell, Shaw, and Simon, 1962), can by appropriate methods be trained (Covington and Crutchfield, 1965).

A second condition necessary for benefiting creatively from fantasy is that the fantasy be at least occasionally relevant to a problem. In the present formulation fantasy content of a certain kind is potentiated by a corresponding current concern, that is, an interrupted, emotionally important operant sequence whose goal has not been abandoned. The mere objective existence of a problem is therefore insufficient to induce relevant fantasy. The individual must still be involved in solving the problem, enough so that relevant cues can elicit the affective responses and their associated subselves and meaning-complexes with sufficient intensity to become regnant. Virtually all descriptions of the stages of a creative act speak of a necessary first stage of "preparation" or "immersion"—a probably long period of concerted struggling with the problem in an effort to solve it.

A further implication of this condition is that the problem-solver must be able to tolerate or even to seek out problems complex enough to require creative solutions. Subjects rated as relatively original prefer greater complexity in their art and in their world (Barron, 1968; Golann, 1962).

A third condition is the provision of opportunities for respondent processes to occur. The importance of this condition probably depends on the type of creative act in question. Some of the creativity of a psychotherapist, debator, teacher, parent, or committee member necessarily occurs in the heat of interaction with others. Those creative solutions that emerge perhaps owe much to the individual's use of his intuitive capacities, the use of his concurrent respondent affects and images. However, autobiographical records of major conceptual creations in the arts and sciences, such as those collected by Ghiselin (1952) and Rugg (1963), seem almost invariably to place the time of insight during what Rugg calls a period of "relaxed tension [p. 11]" when the creator is ostensibly involved in mostly respondent ideation, perhaps during well-integrated motor activity such as walking, shaving, or chatting with a friend. Hypnagogic revery and even sleep have occasioned major creative insights. The solution comes but is not forced. This respondent period forms the usual second stage in descriptions of the creative act, often under the label "stage of incubation." Incubation presumably requires a certain degree of uninvolvement with emotionally tumultuous extraneous events. It is therefore unsurprising that creative scientists have been found to be less gregarious than others (McClelland, 1956; Stein, 1956).

A fourth condition for turning fantasy to creative purposes requires that it be received hospitably. Individuals vary widely in their reception of their own impulses, affects, and ideas. Reception is a complex matter, however, that includes at least two largely independent dimensions (Chapter 11), the inclination to attend to or report them and the disposition to exploit them fully in thought and social interaction.

The inclination to report one's inner turmoil seems to constitute one of the chief differential dimensions of personality (Bendig, 1960; Byrne, 1964). The tendency to admit inner turmoil reflects something other than simply the presence of turmoil, for subjects who score high on the relevant test dimension—often called "anxiety," "neuroticism," or "maladjustment," but in this context "sensitization"—report greater experienced discomfort under threat than low scorers but display less physiological reactivity as measured by skin conductance (Hare, 1966; Lazarus and Alfert, 1964). The dimension of attending to inner events therefore represents tolerance for them and perhaps the learned capacity to utilize them.

In the case of creative problem-solving attending entails both awareness of the content itself and the inclination to scan it for possible application to problems. The "flash of insight" probably requires an attitude of readiness to make connections across the boundary of respondent and operant modes. The flash is "transliminal" in that sense, to use Rugg's (1963) term in a way somewhat different from his. The attitude or personality trait that facilitates transliminality is probably very similar to what Rogers (1959) has called "openness to experience" and lies at the root of the Rogerian capacity for "congruence" between the individual's real, organismic experience and his symbolic formulation of that experience to himself and to others.

The state of receptivity to one's respondent experiences has never been experimentally related to creative activity, but a considerable body of correlational data supports the validity of the theory that relates them. People rated as relatively creative are less swayed than are others by judgments in conflict with their own (Crutchfield, 1962) and are by their own and others' descriptions more fluent, assertive, expressive and unconventional (Barron, 1957); and observations of behavior and projective test responses suggest that creative subjects are better able to integrate, control, and act on their most basic impulses. When creative chemists were shown Rorschach inkblots tachistoscopically at very brief exposure times, they more often responded with interpretations of them than did less creative chemists. They therefore made more "autistic" responses, but they also made more well-formed interpretations than their less creative colleagues (Stein and Meer, 1954). Creative subjects in art were able to produce more idiosyncratic associates than others matched in age, education, intelligence, and sex, were more attracted to "unregulated," flexible, self-assertive personalities, and found greater enjoyment in taking a Rorschach inkblot test (Wild, 1965). Artists who let respondent processes guide them in the formulation of a drawing problem produced more original drawings than artists who conceived of the problem in terms of preconceived categories (Csikszentmihalyi and Getzels, 1970). To summarize, creative individuals not only attend to their respondent processes but value, trust, and actively exploit them.

All in all, then, the model of creative thinking that emerges from the present respondent-process theory of fantasy is consistent with available evidence concerning creative acts and creative persons.

RECAPITULATION OF THE ARGUMENT

The present chapter set out to describe the mode by which fantasys segments are linked and sequenced. A segment was defined as a behavioral or experiential interval homogeneous in thematic content. Homogeneity may occur at different levels of generality, and segments may be organized hierarchically. At the simplest levels, segments were construed as integrated response sequences in the sense of that term developed in the previous chapter: a behavior sequence that unfolds smoothly and automatically, requires little conscious attention to its formation, and requires at most routine processing of stimulus feedback.

Response integration was shown to be somewhat unstable, its cohesiveness subject to the levels of several variables associated with activation. The content of a fantasy segment may therefore be organized in many different ways. A fantasy segment may at one extreme contain operant-like content or it may at the other extreme contain a succession of hallucinatory images whose operant properties are at best vestigial. In fantasy, however, the operant-like content is functionally nonoperant. It is elicited involuntarily by antecedent cues, and its termination is dependent not on goal-attainment or goal-related criteria but on its interruption by a new fantasy segment, which was in turn elicited by cues that were very probably generated by the interrupted segment.

Concern with sequencing, then, is in this chapter concern with sequencing *of segments*. In this regard, fantasy was portrayed as a respondent sequence of segments, much as problem solving is an operant sequence. The respondent-operant distinction as applied to modes of sequencing parallels the Freudian distinction between primary and secondary process in a number of crucial ways. Like primary process behavior, respondent behavior entails the involuntary elicitation of behavior rather than its deliberate emission, is unconcerned with impact on the environment, makes little or no use of feedback in the guiding of responses, is normally controlled by the events that precede its onset rather than by response-contingent consequences, is likely to be described in terms of response topography rather than of its final effects on the environment, and seems phenomenologically effortless.

Earlier chapters make the distinction between two kinds of determinants of fantasy content. One kind is regarded as a relatively long-term determinant, encompassing periods of hours, days, or even longer. This class of potentiating factors is recognized in such concepts as unconscious wish, need, drive, motive, etc., and is formulated in Chapter 3 as "current concern." This class of longer-term determinants is considered at length in Chapters 8 to 11. However, a second kind of determinant is necessary to account for the flow of fantasy segments, a determinant of the moment-to-moment shifts in content.

The argument of the present chapter has been directed at elucidating this shorter-term determinant. Consideration of the problem of respondent linkages suggested that gross shifts in content can best be conceptualized as shifts in the regnancy of affectively-toned dispositional self-states, here called "subselves." Finer shifts in content may occur within the same sub-self, and these shifts too are ushered in with affective arousal. Arousal, however, may be relatively unobtrusive, as in the case of vestigial orient-ing reactions. Thus affective arousal forms the leading edge of a newly elicited segment and subself. Newly regnant subselves are in this concep-tion always accompanied by the beginning of a new segment, although new segments need not require the initiation of a newly regnant subself. In ei-ther case, cues embedded in an experiential process at one moment in time elicit an affect and associated other responses (e.g., verbal and imaginal re-sponses) which constitute a new segment, which may unfold until its content, in turn, elicits another affectively-toned integrated tendency, and so on. The cues that elicit new respondent segments may do so simply be-cause they are unexpected. However, current concerns potentiate affective responses to concern-related cues, and this seems likely to provide the nor-mal mechanism for the initiation of new segments.

In actuality respondent and operant modes of sequencing are frequently intermixed. Respondent processes may give rise to operant activity, and operant activity may give way to respondent interludes. The intermixture may take the form of long periods of largely operant activity followed by long periods of largely respondent activity, or it may take the form of re-spondent activity which occurs concurrently with operant activity and acts as a channel of information into the operant stream. The first pattern of intermixture has been characteristically associated with acts of major con-ceptual creativity. The second pattern corresponds to intuitive, original, or successfully divergent thinking. Creative acts occur when respondent seg-ments elicited by cues that are nonobviously related to the solution of a problem bring useful new elements into juxtaposition with old response schemas. However, in order for an individual to benefit from his respon-dent channel he must possess relevant and competent response segments, generate opportunities for appropriate respondent activity to take place, and exploit the results of respondent activity. These conditions, derived from the present theoretical system, emerge consistently in empirical stud-ies of creative individuals.

PART IV

Determinants of the Content of Fantasy

CHAPTER 8

Motivational Effects on Fantasy: A Theoretical Framework

The sequencing of fantasy segments can be thought of as determined by two different kinds of factors at two different levels of specificity. First, one can think of the momentary events that take place when one particular segment terminates or is interrupted and is replaced by the next particular segment. That is the level of analysis employed in the preceding chapter. Second, one can think of rather more enduring factors that predispose a person to engage in fantasy intermittently about some particular class of content over some period of time—a few minutes, hours, or days. By themselves the latter factors determine the relative *frequency* with which a person fantasizes about a class of content, but are unconcerned with the mechanism of segment-to-segment shifts.

Both kinds of determinants can include the kinds of events that have been labeled "motivational." Furthermore if an enduring disposition is ever to be translated into a concrete momentary response the two kinds of factors must interact in some way to produce modulations in the stream of behavior. Studies of fantasy have rarely focused on the naturally-occurring unfolding of responses, but the operation of relatively longer-term motivational determinants on fantasy has been the object of a venerable research history, employing as dependent variables primarily content ratings of projective-test protocols, especially TAT stories.

It is this class of determinants that Chapters 8 to 11 consider, both the evidence that has accumulated and the theoretical questions to which it gives rise. What factors lead a person to engage in frequent achievement fantasy or power fantasy? What are the effects on fantasy of hunger, anger, or uncompleted tasks? What elements of antecedent conditions produce effects, and on which features of the resulting fantasy responses?

The present chapter considers the nature of what is meant by motivation, and then pulls together from the burgeoning literature of motivational

praised socially creates social risks and seems likely in these experimental situations to have set in motion concerns and perhaps stratagems for winning approval and for avoiding or remedying rejection. Since the social payoff of these affiliative incentives would occur after the experimental period when the subjects had resumed their normal social interaction, the relevant concern spans the time period into which the experimenters had interpolated the writing of TAT stories. Thus the TAT stories ought to reflect the aroused affiliative concerns. All three of the investigations indeed obtained significantly raised n Aff scores after the sociometric arousal procedure.

Two of the investigations included pertinent additional evidence. Shipley and Veroff (1952) compared a group of freshman who had been accepted into fraternities with a second group who had been rejected. Since the subjects had not, of course, been randomly assigned to conditions, the interpretation of the results cannot be unequivocal, but it is nevertheless interesting that when tested a month after the rushing period, the rejected group scored significantly higher in TAT n Aff. Rosenfeld and Franklin (1966) provided comparable results in the framework of the experimental design described above that did permit random assignment of subjects to conditions. They added two "feedback" groups to the groups described above. The women of one group were informed after a ten-minute musical interlude following their ratings that they had been rated favorably by their dormitory-mates, and the members of the other group were told that they had been rated unfavorably. The feedback was followed by the TAT. From the standpoint of present theory, the members of the "liked" group were provided with the attainment of their affiliative reward, while the "disliked" subjects were provided not only with an immediate punishment but also with the prospect, an incentive, of becoming better liked, provided they could muster the social skills to bring it about. Positive feedback thus in effect terminated a concern, while negative feedback protracted or instated one. In accordance with the present formulation the "disliked" women produced the highest n Aff scores of any group, while the n Aff scores of the "liked" women were slightly elevated but not significantly higher than those of the nonaroused control group.

Another variable of fantasy content that has attracted systematic attention is the need for power (n Power), which Veroff (1958) described as concern with "the control of the means of influencing a person [p. 220]." Experimental investigations of n Power are hard to come by, however. Veroff (1957) reported the results of testing candidates for student office on election eve while they were awaiting election returns. In comparison with a group of captive subjects taking an undergraduate course, the political group wrote stories significantly more saturated with n Power. The two groups can by no stretch of the imagination be considered comparable, of course, but the results are consistent with the present position.

Walker and Atkinson (1958) investigated the effect of a sharply fear-evoking experience on fantasies of fear and avoidance. They obtained TAT stories from soldiers at five time intervals before, during, and after their being stationed 4000 yards from the detonation of a nuclear device: long before the explosion at another camp, 10 hours before, one half hour before at the site, 10 hours after, and two weeks later. At the first time point the subjects were unaware of the nuclear project. Compared with the TAT stories at that time, TAT stories at all but the last point contained significantly more fear-related content.

The rise in fearful fantasy before the explosion is clearly consistent with the present formulation. However, fear, more than needs for achievement, affiliation, power, etc., has compelling physiological correlates, the kind of physiological arousal that fits the concept of "drive." Drive, as we have seen, is best treated as having some distinctive effects beyond those of incentive properties. The complexities of the effects of fear or anxiety have been ably explored by Epstein (1967) and his colleagues. He obtained a significant portion of the evidence for his theory of anxiety from studies of fear in parachutists, including the effects of parachuting on TAT stories (Fenz and Epstein, 1962). They found, consistent with the present formulation, that parachutists tell more stories favorable to parachuting before a jump than after, and more such stories than nonparachutists. Unexpectedly, the parachutists on the day of a jump expressed less fear of parachuting than they did later or than other subjects, although they produced more fear responses, presumably displaced, that were irrelevant to parachuting, and also more hostility.

The drive aspects of fear and their effects on fantasy are considered in greater depth in Chapter 10. For present purposes, however, it seems clear that the positive incentive of parachuting is reflected in positive TAT stories about parachuting during the time when the subject has decided to jump and is preparing for the occasion. To explain the remarkable pattern of avoidance responses, Epstein has proposed a two-factor theory of anxiety in which gradients of fear arousal summate with gradients of inhibition of fear. In the language of the present theoretical position, however, it makes sense to suppose that the activity of jumping from a plane entails an organized constellation of cognitive, motor, and affective responses—a "parachuting subself"—which, like other subselves, carries with it the potentiation of associated processes and the inhibition of alien ones. If the parachuting subself is regnant during the day of a jump, pro-parachuting fantasy ought to be potentiated and responses of fleeing from parachuting ought to be attenuated. Fenz and Epstein reported that some parachutists deny fear on the day of the jump, and on that day these also display less physiological arousal than do other parachutists. At other times, other subselves are likely to be regnant, and in some of these states the parachutist may be better able to experience fear of parachuting, perhaps even becoming aghast at his own recklessness in parachuting.

Other forms of stress, which are less voluntary and less a focus of the organization of a personality, seem to creep directly into fantasy, as the nuclear results gathered by Walker and Atkinson suggest. It is assumed here that stress responses are avoidance responses to negative incentives. Barton (1964) gave a set of TAT-like pictures to children entering a general medical hospital on the day of admission and the day before discharge. Their responses were compared with a control sample approximately matched for age, sex, and father's occupation. The hospitalized children told stories significantly more imbued with dependency, fear, and defense. Since subjects were obviously not assigned to conditions randomly, it is impossible to estimate how much personality factors or experiences other than the immediate hospitalization may have contributed to these differences. It is known that many more of the hospitalized children had had previous experiences with hospitalization than had the control children. However, the TAT stress responses of the hospitalized children increased significantly more from intake to discharge than those of the controls at comparable intervals, a fact less readily explained by factors of personality or previous history.

All in all, then, the available evidence seems unfalteringly in support of the proposition that being engaged in behavior relative to an effective incentive potentiates corresponding fantasy content. A small amount of additional evidence suggests that upon attainment of a positive incentive the concern ends and fantasy relevant to the incentive declines.

EFFECTS OF INTERRUPTION ON FANTASY

Behavior, as we have seen, tends to become organized into integrated response sequences, and one or a succession of these tend to be emitted upon the occasion of expecting incentives of certain appropriate kinds under certain auspicious conditions. In the absence of other factors, goal-directed behavior sequences run to completion. In reality, however, they are often interrupted, for a variety of reasons. A goal-directed sequence might be superceded by the sudden intrusion of a more powerful incentive that requires activity incompatible with the first. Circumstances might require a temporary interruption: fatigue; the need to wait for another person's cooperative action; time required for an instrumental act to take effect, as in mailing a love letter; etc. A sequence might encounter an insuperable, unexpected obstacle that prevents an organism from continuing his pursuit of a goal. Experimental studies of interruption have investigated the effects of obstacles on memory, affect, arousal, persistence, and, in a few indirect cases, on TAT fantasy.

Interruption is actually an integral part of basic psychology, for it encompasses many common procedures and concepts. Major theoretical systems have incorporated it in central positions, sometimes explicitly and sometimes with direct implications for fantasy and thought. In elaborating perhaps the first quantitative theory of psychology, Herbart (1834) wrote that "the flow of concepts ["Vorstellungen," often translated as "ideas"] stops and expands at the point which is desired and not immediately reached. The reproductions awakened by it are collected (at first without order) as fancies [Phantasien] . . . [Pp. 184–185]." Thus fantasy begins *in lieu* of reaching a goal. In Freudian theory, the development of reality-oriented "secondary process" in thinking and action occurs as a result of the inadequacy of the infant's primitive response systems to achieve gratification. The role of the ego is, indeed, to interrupt the attainment of gratification productively, to ensure that it will eventually occur. When secondary process fails, the organism reverts to activities governed by primary process: dreams, hallucinations, and fantasy.

Interruption is widely thought to heighten drive or emotion. In Hullian theory, drive grows in strength when the organism is blocked from reducing it. In the instrumental learning theories of Thorndike, Hull, Skinner, and their theoretical heirs, the concept of extinction inherently entails the interruption of goal-striving before the emission of a goal response. Mowrer (1950) and others have defined anxiety operationally as the response to helplessness in the face of impending pain, an interruption of avoidance or escape. The interruption of appetitive goal-striving comes to define the concept of frustration (Dollard, Doob, Miller, Mowrer, and Sears, 1939). Amsel (1958) subsequently wedded the extinguishing and frustrating aspects of interruption in the theoretical concept of "frustrative nonreward." Lewin (1935) constructed a "dynamic" psychology whose "needs," "tensions," and "forces" could be demonstrated operationally only by interrupting subjects in some way.

Clearly the phenomenon of interruption pervades much of psychology. Relatively recent partial reviews are available elsewhere. Butterfield (1964) has reviewed the effects and correlates of interrupting subjects' task behavior; Mandler (1964) surveyed the problem broadly and added significant data concerning the emotional and cognitive consequences of interruption.

Mandler's work bears summarizing. First, he set forth a theoretical position based on previous work:

"I suggest that the interruption of an organized response produces a state of arousal which, in the absence of completion or substitution, then develops into one or another emotional expression, depending upon the occasion of the interruption [p. 174]. . . . It is interesting to speculate that all organized responses may act as inhibitors and that visceral arousal is a necessary consequence of the withdrawal of an inhibitor—and thus the antecedent for emotional behavior [pp. 175–176]."

Second, Mandler added the results of new investigations. Both rats and human subjects displayed emotional behavior under extinction. When rats who had overlearned a maze and presumably had integrated the maze-running response were compared with rats who had barely mastered it, the rats who had overlearned the maze behaved somewhat differently at extinction, including greater sniffing. Mandler suggested that "sniffing is an index of exploratory behavior" and "indicates a search for substitute behavior when a well-organized sequence has been interrupted [p. 194]."

The implication, of course, is that the interrupted sequence continues to have some sort of psychological reality after the interruption, that the concern continues. That agrees with Lewin's theory and with Zeigarnik's (1927) prototypical finding that subjects are more likely to recall interrupted than completed tasks. Atkinson (1953) refined Zeigarnik's result by showing that recall of incomplete tasks is related to subjects' TAT n Ach in interaction with instructions, as described above. The Atkinson results constitute a qualification of Zeigarnik's and are amenable to the interpretation that subjects recall more incomplete tasks when the act of completing the task is or leads to an incentive appropriate to the subjects' role as they perceive it. However, before one could consider the Zeigarnik effect to support the notion of a continuing concern one would have to assume that improved recall of tasks arises from continued concern. The assumption is by no means obvious, since people retain much material that does not concern them currently. Zeigarnik's and Atkinson's subjects recalled many of the tasks they had completed. Increased recall can therefore represent improved original learning (Caron and Wallach, 1959) or improved fixation of the memory as well as the continued currency of a relevant concern. Any effects produced because the subject's current concern potentiates memories of the unfinished tasks must be superimposed on other effects on memory. Thus the recall of tasks is potentially a highly complex phenomenon which remains incompletely analyzed after nearly half a century of sporadic investigation.

Direct, deliberate investigations of the effects of interruption on fantasy are rare indeed. Such studies are sorely needed to pinpoint the conditions under which effects occur. Fortunately, however, other kinds of studies of fantasy provide some information; for example, all of the investigations on effects of incentives reviewed in the previous section are relevant, since all of the experiments in which positive effects of incentives could be demonstrated achieved those effects by interpolating the TAT or similar procedures between the introduction of incentives and the completion of the incentive-related activity, thereby interrupting the goal-directed instrumental activity. The conclusion reached there applies here too: interruption of behavior directed at incentives produces fantasy content that corresponds thematically to the content of the interrupted sequence.

Other studies produced interruption in such a way as deliberately to create "frustration," that is, an emotional response that would eventuate in anger. Since anger, in the somewhat arbitrary classification used here, appears to have intrinsic drive properties, these investigations are examined in Chapter 10.

FACTORS THAT GOVERN THE EFFECTIVENESS OF INCENTIVES

If incentive is defined as an objective feature of a situation—the size or type of reward, for instance—then it is necessary to distinguish between incentive and incentive value. If one man's meat is another man's poison, one is hard pressed to predict a man's behavior knowing only that the reward is a certain object. One needs to know more in order to estimate the value a man will place on the incentive.

Certainly the objective properties of incentives are of crucial importance when predicting their effects on performance. The quality of an incentive and its amount have been shown repeatedly to affect the vigor of performance by animals (Cofer and Appley, 1964). Studies of their effects on fantasy have apparently not been attempted, and should be, but it seems likely that trivial incentives lack influence over fantasy processes. In addition to the properties of the incentive object itself, however, a number of other factors influence performance: the expected delay of reward, the spatial or temporal distance between the subject and his goal, the probability that he can attain the goal, and the amount of effort already expended. Little research is available on the influence of these variables in moderating the effects of incentives on fantasy. There have been many investigations of the way in which subjects' expectancy of success affects their performance in various undertakings, and these studies commonly employed TAT *n* Ach or fear of failure scores (Atkinson, 1964; Klinger and McNelly, 1969), but Atkinson's theoretical framework, within which this work has been done, is unlikely to raise major questions about the effect of expectancy on fantasy itself. One experiment that did investigate the effect of expectancy of success on achievement fantasy (Murstein and Collier, 1962) found no differential effects.

Social Role Effects

At least one other, more complicated class of factors affects how much incentives will potentiate fantasy content: the subject's social role. Every individual in a social order occupies a status—a set of social norms about him which consist of certain expectations concerning his behavior and certain standards or guides for perceiving and interpreting it. His role is the behavior pattern expected of him. An individual's enactment of his role is supported and controlled by socially administered incentives for appropriate behavior, and it develops as the behavioral product of operant shaping processes applied by his parents, authorities, and peers. The individual's realization that the people around him can invoke sanctions against his deviations from role-appropriate behavior serves as an implicit or explicit incentive for him to avoid deviation. Each role thus comes to suggest and delimit an individual's permissible aspirations, rewards, strategies, and acts in each particular kind of social context, and also specifies a number of role-inappropriate aspirations, rewards, strategies, and acts.

Except for studies of achievement fantasy in TAT stories, the evidence of social status effects on fantasy is at best scattered and weak, but insofar as it exists it suggests that status effects are important. Social status may affect the frequency with which people engage in daydream forms of fantasy. At least black, Italian, and Jewish New York students report a higher frequency of daydreams than do New York students of Anglo-Saxon, German, or Irish extraction (Singer and McCraven, 1962). Since the reports were obtained retrospectively by having subjects rate the frequency of their daydreams of various kinds, the differences between ethnic groups could be explained in a variety of ways: actual differences in the frequency of daydreaming, differences in attention to daydreams, differences in retention of daydreams, or response-set differences in the willingness to report daydreams. However, taken at face value, the data confirm Singer and McCraven's hypothesis that upwardly mobile groups such as blacks, Italians, and Jews daydream more than more securely established groups, presumably because they face more challenges and changes in the course of climbing up the socioeconomic ladder. That hypothesis accords also to some extent with the present position. Groups with more problems which are emotionally involving, or groups with more important incentives before them, have more current concerns which potentiate corresponding fantasy. It is not clear however, that the larger number of kinds of daydreams reported means a greater amount of fantasy generally. Given the limitations of Singer's Daydream Questionnaire, the evidence on the frequency with which people indulge in respondent activity must be considered inconclusive.

Singer and McCraven's data also suggest some differences between the ethnic groups in the content of the daydreams. Thus the blacks, Italians, and Jews reported a higher frequency of erotic daydreams. Again taking the data at face value, the finding would indirectly support the suggestion that the kinds of daydreams of upwardly mobile individuals arise from the many problems they encounter, which they may be at times experience as severe frustrations. The explanation runs as follows. Frustrations lead at least much of the time to the arousal of aggression. Aroused aggression spills over into fantasy—at least TAT fantasy—but it does so in a way that raises not only aggressive fantasy but also sexual fantasy (Barclay and Haber, 1965). Hence a higher incidence of erotic fantasy in an ethnic group may reflect the greater degree of aggression aroused by its members' life circumstances in New York. Despite the esthetically pleasing qualities of such an explanation, the data could be regarded as consistent with a more mundane interpretation, that erotic ideation is more readily accepted by the members of the upwardly mobile groups described and is therefore more readily experienced and reported.

The latter interpretation would be consistent with the evidence concerning a kind of fantasy about which much more is known, achievement fantasy in TAT stories. The pattern of evidence strongly suggests that the content of fantasy reflects an individual's current social status, and that it does so because status dictates the incentives that an individual may permit himself to covet which, in turn, presumably determines his current concerns (Klinger and McNelly, 1969). The relationship is seen most clearly when subjects' tendency to incorporate n Ach in their TAT stories is examined in relation to their performance levels in various kinds of task situations and in relation to the kinds of challenges they prefer to face. Subjects who score high in n Ach perceive themselves as normally overcoming relatively challenging odds in achievement situations, where the probability of success is for instance about .3. They prefer situations of that kind, and work harder and more effectively there. In contrast, subjects who score low in n Ach perceive themselves as undertaking relatively unchallenging, humdrum tasks that normally carry low status. They prefer such situations in which the probability of success is high (say, .7) although they also sometimes prefer odds so unrealistically low (say, .1) that the undertaking is in the spirit of a foredoomed enterprise. Subjects low in n Ach work hardest and most effectively in these relatively safe achievement situations that are unlikely to produce many strong achievement concerns. Since n Ach is relatively unstable, and since its incidence changes with changes in current social status, it seems likely that status determines the level of achievement fantasy, rather than n Ach determining status. One may conclude that the relationship between status and fantasy arises because of the kinds of undertakings which a person's status permits him to launch, or at least which his perception and acceptance of his status encompasses. Since undertakings are presumably governed by effective net incentives, the status that determines undertakings must have done so by determining the subject's valuation of various incentives, which in turn determine his current concerns, which, finally, determine the content of his fantasy.

The extent to which social roles moderate the effects of incentives on fantasy can also be seen clearly in another corner of the evidence on achievement fantasy, that corner concerned with achievement fantasy in women. All of the preceding evidence from research on achievement fantasy was evidence obtained with male subjects. Early attempts to replicate the evidence with women came to naught and were abandoned for a time in puzzlement. A series of investigations subsequently laid bare the reasons for the failures: most women in our society play roles which in contrast to male roles prescribe markedly more circumscribed achievements directed toward quite different incentives. As a result, the experimental operations which successfully implied intrinsic incentives to American men implied no such thing for most of the women.

The most striking evidence that this is so came in a report by French and Lesser (1964) concerning the arousal of n Ach in college women. The measure of n Ach was obtained from responses to the French Test of Insight. There were two kinds of arousal conditions, both contained in instructions that preceded the Test of Insight but were directed at a task that was to follow it. One, an "intellectual" arousal condition similar to that commonly employed with men, presented a scrambled words task as a measure of intelligence, performance on which would reflect not only on the subject but also on her college. The other, a "woman's role" arousal condition, presented a "social skills test" as a predictor of how successful a subject would be in attaining the goal of a "successful marriage, children, and a full and happy family and social life," a goal presented as "very important" to "most girls." At an earlier session, each subject had answered a "value orientation" questionnaire that assessed her view of the importance of intellectual and "woman's role" goals to women at her college, and asked the subject if she personally agreed with the prevailing norms. Thus subjects could be grouped according to whether they strongly held prominent intellectual goals but weak feminine ones, strong "woman's-role" goals but weak intellectual ones, or strong goals of both kinds. The upshot of the study was that while both kinds of arousal raised n Ach in most groups of subjects, intellectual arousal was most effective with intellectually inclined women and "woman's-role" arousal was most effective with women inclined to the "woman's role." Indeed, "woman's-role" arousal actually depressed n Ach below the level of a neutral condition in women who expressed strong intellectual goals but weak "woman's-role" goals. The depression of n Ach suggests that the instructions, which seemed to support "woman's-role" goals, may have aroused conflict, guilt feelings, or anxiety about achievement in women who were exclusively intellectually inclined.

The results of French and Lesser are very similar in form to those of Glass (1957). With men who characteristically fear failure, arousal instructions that emphasized avoiding failure raised TAT n Ach more than did instructions which emphasized hope of success; whereas with unanxious subjects the failure instructions lowered n Ach scores below the level of n Ach produced by instructions that emphasized hope of success. In this case as in the case of gender role, arousal has its greatest effect on fantasy when the incentives it implies are consistent with the subject's perception of his role. When the implied incentives are inconsistent, the subject acts in fantasy as though the apparent incentives were worthless to him or even aversive.

The discussion so far has focused on the effects exerted by social roles on the kinds of incentives people value and therefore on the kinds of content about which they fantasy. Social roles may also, however, influence the value of material incentives in general and the strength of all of an individual's current concerns. Mystics who strive to experience profound meditation must try to eliminate the ideational distractions which make up normal fantasy. The meditative experience is therefore antithetical to the experience of free fantasy. In order to facilitate meditation, mystic groups recognize the value of "renunciation" (Deikman, 1969), of abandoning worldly incentives and entering a life of perpetual poverty, chastity, and solitude. The effect of such a life seems to be to lessen the imperiousness of all an individual's current concerns, thus helping the mystic to keep his consciousness free of intrusions during deep meditation.

Uncertainty of Outcome

In a view expressed a decade ago (Miller, Galanter, and Pribram, 1960), people are forever in the process of following a plan—often, indeed, several intertwined plans—and in the framework of incentive theory are therefore at all times behaving in relation to one or more incentives. As people strive after incentives, incentives play on people, sensitizing them to particular experiences and creating concerns that color the content of their thoughts and respondent activities.

It seems unlikely, however, that all concerns potentiate fantasies equally. Concerns regarding emotionally important incentives no doubt (although there are few data) command fantasy more effectively than trivial ones. Apart from differences in the importance of incentives, however, there appears to be another relevant factor, the degree of the person's certainty that he can attain the incentive.

Degree of certainty, or the subject's expectancy concerning success, has figured prominently in the motivational theories of instrumental behavior proposed by Atkinson (1964) and his predecessors. There, the greater the expectancy of success, the greater the tendency to seek the incentive, except when in the case of achievement incentives too great a chance of success may reduce the value of the incentive in the subject's estimation. If incentive value and expectancy of success are independent, however, the degree of certainty that success can be achieved directly determines the tendency to seek the reward.

Atkinson's theory has been applied almost exclusively to achievement behavior, and its application to fantasy has correspondingly been confined to achievement fantasy. It is precisely with achievement incentives—the intrinsic pleasure of accomplishment against a standard of excellence— that incentive value is not independent of expectancy, and, in fact, Atkinson proposed that they are exactly complementary. If P is the subjective probability of success in a task, its incentive value is $1-P$. Atkinson theorized that the effective attractiveness of an incentive, leaving aside for the moment the subject's enduring motivational disposition toward it, is the product $P(1-P)$. The product is greatest when $P=.5$; that is, a person is most impelled to seek an achievement reward when its attainment is most uncertain, midway between a sure bet and an impossibility. Although there is reason to believe that the most compelling rewards may have probabilities of success less than or greater than .5, depending on the attributes of particular subjects (Heckhausen, 1968; Klinger and McNelly, 1969), the general theoretical approach has worked well in the prediction of behavior.

The present theory of fantasy leads to grossly similar conclusions concerning achievement fantasy: it is most likely when the subject is engaged in an achievement concern and the outcome is uncertain. However, the present position rests on a different set of reasons and extends the generalization to incentives other than achievement.

We may consider separately three cases, one in which the probability of a successful outcome $P=0$, a second in which $P=1.0$, and a third in which P is intermediate. In the first case, in which the reward is completely inaccessible, no incentive exists in effect, and no current concern can be mobilized. Such a situation is found in cases where drive is high but incentive has been foresworn or placed out of reach. The second case is more complicated. In many instances of rewards, whatever response led to their being certain is for practical purposes a goal-attaining response. Certainty of attaining rewards is tantamount to accomplishment and virtually ends the current concern. Few salaried tenured employees are likely to be concerned over the receipt of their next regular paycheck, and few probably entertain fantasies about obtaining it. However, there are some kinds of incentives whose delay may protract unpleasant drive states, even though the eventual delivery of the incentive is assured, as in hunger before a late meal. It seems likely that if the meal is virtually certain to be served at the promised time the sheer prospect of eating it will mobilize few fantasies, although the drive stimuli associated with hunger may attract recurrent attention and perhaps fantasy. Data on the precise effects of assured incentives on fantasy are lacking and are badly needed. One would wish to know, for instance, what are the effects of food deprivation when the subject knows exactly the time and menu of the next meal; and it would be helpful to perform such a study with the intensity of drive stimuli masked or attenuated.

Omitting for the moment the difficult case in which drive stimuli nag the individual after he has already assured himself of later satisfaction, the most potent determiners of fantasy seem to be concerns over incentives that are neither assured nor unattainable but somewhere in between: the venture still in the planning stage, the examination in the offing or already taken but not yet graded, the girl who has so far said only "maybe," the blunder which the boss has yet to discover, the invitation that may be tendered, the promotion that may come soon. As the direction of the outcome becomes plainer, its hold on fantasy should become weaker. That may account for the progressive impoverishment of fantasy between adolescence and middle adulthood (Singer, 1966) as fantasy themes become increasingly bound to the adult's conception of his reality, a reality that often seems incredibly constricted, colorless, and pessimistic to the young.

It may seem that the generalization ventured here, that potent concerns are directed at uncertain outcomes, is contradicted by the widely believed but little-documented tendency of the elderly to reminisce. After all, reminiscences are manifestly devoted to bygone events whose outcome is known and to the pursuit of now-defunct incentives. Reminiscence in old age is nevertheless consistent with the present theory. Current concerns set the topics for fantasy but the fantasy process is a respondent chain subjected in varying degrees to symbolic transformations. Concern with an incentive is more than a rumination about the incentive itself, although incentive-*related* themes are potentiated thereby. Some reminiscence therefore creeps into everyone's fantasies, since particular memories rele-

ply. Pytkowicz et al. also asked their subjects to describe their own levels of hostility after the other experimental procedures, and found to their surprise that subjects described themselves as less hostile after the cognitive task than after a fantasy period. In light of this datum one might have speculated that, during fantasy, subjects continued to mull their anger and hence regarded themselves as more hostile at the end of the fantasy condition, but, contrary to Feshbach's data, Pytkowicz found no differences in the aggression that insulted and noninsulted subjects expressed in their TAT stories. There is yet another speculative explanation. Perhaps some subjects felt that the bald insults directed at them justified their anger, and in view of the size of their provocation they rated themselves as less hostile kinds of persons than they would otherwise, since "hostile" people are those who respond with disproportionately great hostility *relative to* the size of the provocations. Such an explanation would apply to Pytkowicz's results only if the task kept subjects angrier and more self-justified than the fantasy activity did. As we shall see, there is reason to suppose that that is what happened.

Lesser (1962) angered boys aged seven to nine by inducing them to fail a task and by depriving them of a favorite toy. Her criterion measure of outcome was aggressiveness in subsequent free play. There were three groups of subjects, one of whom wrote TAT stories during the interval between frustration and play, a second engaged in a matching task, and the third had no interval at all. Their play contained more aggression after the task than after either the TAT or no interval at all. Subjects after no interval expressed no more aggression than after the TAT. After no interval or after the TAT, aggression gradually subsided during the free play period. After the task, aggression remained high throughout the free play period.

Can one conclude that, after a subject is angered, tasks increase aggression? Apart from Lesser's evidence, Berkowitz (1960) suggested that the tasks might serve as continuing irritants to insulted subjects, repeatedly reminding them of the affront, whereas subjects are inclined to lose themselves in other concerns during the process of fantasying. He devised a task especially designed to remind subjects of their anger and found that it indeed raised subjects' later hostility over the level produced after writing TAT stories, which had remained essentially unchanged from a pre-TAT measure of subjects' hostility.

It is important to understand clearly what such an explanation does and does not mean. It does suggest that provoked aggression is less likely to be acted upon after a period of fantasy than after a period of working on a cognitive task for the provocateur. If the universe of behavior is divided into two classes of behavior, fantasy and nonfantasy, then if nonfantasy behavior can be said to maintain aggression relative to fantasy behavior, fantasy can equally well be said to reduce the tendency to aggression relative to nonfantasy behavior. However, the finding that fantasy yields less behavioral tendency to aggression than performing a task does is not tantamount to the statement that it reduces drive, and it does not suggest by what psychological mechanism the behavioral change is effected.

That fantasy does not in fact reduce drive levels now seems clear on the basis of psychophysiological evidence. When subjects are frustrated and angered they experience a rise in systolic blood pressure. If they are permitted to aggress physically or verbally against their frustrator, their blood pressure quickly drops again, but it remains high if they engage only in fantasy instead of overt aggression (Baker and Schaie, 1969; Hokanson & Burgess, 1962). Indeed, blood pressure tends to remain elevated for a time even after the subject has had the opportunity to aggress overtly, if the target was someone other than his frustrator (Hokanson, Burgess, and Cohen, 1963).

None of the studies of fantasy effects on drive levels has investigated the possibility that, after a subject has been angered, administering a nonfantasy task to him might raise his blood pressure even more. It remains conceivable that the effect of fantasy is most prominently to keep anger from rising further, rather than to reduce it.

The set of concepts that has been developed in previous pages to account for the data of fantasy seems also capable of accommodating the rather complex set of results concerning fantasy effects on aggression. In the experimental conditions commonly employed subjects were from their viewpoint victimized by a boorish experimenter against whom the chance for retaliation must have seemed uncertain. Since fantasy content seems to be potentiated by incentive-oriented current concerns, it follows that whether an anger-provocation increases TAT aggression is a measure not of the anger arousal itself but of the extent to which the subjects believe they might be able to vent their anger at the instigator. Since insult conditions raise subjects' TAT aggression at most by a rather small amount, as in Feshbach's case, and since most subjects' fantasies are far from saturated with aggression even after gross insult, one may surmise that for most subjects the prospect of effective retaliation is small. That may be cold comfort from the standpoint of their blood pressure, but it frees their fantasies for other concerns.

One more element is necessary to complete the picture. As we see in Chapter 5, the evocation of fantasy themes probably involves more than a change in ideational content, but involves the evocation of a "subself." Evidence accumulating from our Morris studies, which are more thoroughly described in Chapter 12, suggests that themes and regnant subselves are relatively short-lived in fantasy, giving way rapidly to other content that is thematically unlike the content it replaces. In short, fantasy is a kind of cycling process that facilitates changes in the topic of thought. Of course current concerns potentiate content that corresponds to them, and intense concerns may lead to preoccupation with a narrow range of content, but even strong potentiation does not yield thought that is necessarily exclusively devoted to the concern. Furthermore, whereas current concerns seem to operate in relation to more or less accessible incentives, the prospect that an experimentally insulted subject may vent his anger on the instigator of the anger is probably relatively dim. In these experiments, therefore, a period of fantasy should lead in many cases to a subsidence of subjects' hostile subselves, and hence to a relative weakening of their hostility at the end of the fantasy period. By contrast, a task which keeps the subject reminded of his irritation should help to maintain the regnancy of subjects' hostile subselves, and hence maintain a higher readiness to aggress at the task's end.

Conclusions. To summarize a complex set of data and interpretations:

1. Angered subjects act out less aggression after a period of fantasy than after a period in which they must undertake cognitive tasks that are associated with the instigator of anger. What probably happens is that the tasks serve as continuing reminders of the provocation, whereas in fantasy, which is a kind of content-cycling process, subjects' hostile subselves tend more often to subside, thus holding down or lessening the subject's inclination to aggress.

2. Angered subjects describe themselves as less hostile after tasks than after fantasy, perhaps because the angrier subjects in task conditions perceive their anger to be better justified by the size of the provocation, and hence they feel less disproportionately hostile.

3. Fantasy is incapable of lowering hostile drive levels as such.

4. Angering subjects when they have little chance to retaliate—i.e., when incentives are inaccessible—produces at best small effects on TAT fantasy.

Anxiety and Subject-Produced Fantasy

Anxiety is, of course, a quite different kind of drive from aggression. Whereas aggression is a kind of approach behavior which seeks a positive consummatory response, anxiety and fear are part of avoidance behavior, seeking to avoid an anticipated negative incentive. Whereas aggressive drive is reduced by positive acts of aggression, anxiety is reduced by the cessation of threat. Therefore, in the case of anxiety it makes little sense to speak of discharges of blocked instinctual energies or of drive-reduction in the sense of less desire to avoid a noxious experience. It seems more appropriate to ask what effects fantasy has in soothing the emotionality of people under stress.

Here again one must make a distinction. Stress produced by the anticipation of pain is different from stress produced by having already undergone an unsettling event. In both cases the evidence is extremely thin, but studies by Singer and Rowe provide an indication.

People awaiting pain may experience less anxiety while daydreaming than while engaging in a task. Rowe (1963) strapped subjects down in isolated cubicles and recorded heart rate and GSRs during a series of manipulations. Subjects were led to expect that after certain time periods they would receive electric shock. During these intervals they were either left to wait with nothing to do but think and presumably to daydream, or were given a digit-span task of repeating sets of four digits read to them by the experimenter. Taken as a whole, the digit-span intervals were filled with higher heart rates and GSRs than were the daydream intervals. Toward the ends of the daydream intervals, however, when subjects expected to receive the shocks, their heart rates rose to the same level as during the digit-span task. The results are consistent with the interpretation that, because of the content-cycling effect of fantasy, subjects were less often reminded of their peril during daydreaming than during the continual pelting of experimenter-controlled stimuli in the digit-span task.

Following an unpleasant experience, however, daydreaming may foster increased anxiety. Singer and Rowe (1962) sprang a surprise test on classes of graduate students in education, and afterwards, following an interval of either daydreaming or filling out an attitude questionnaire, gave subjects two anxiety tests. On one of the tests, subjects indicated greater anxiety after daydreaming than after filling out the questionnaire.

The experimental design appears to conform to the requirements for producing unsettling effects, discussed in a previous section. Since the subjects were summer graduate students in education, a surprise test might appear to jeopardize their very careers if they performed poorly enough. In accordance with the earlier analysis of unsettling events, the surprise test would be expected to mobilize concerns over longer-range objectives, whose jeopardy would arouse considerable anxiety, and the daydreaming period would encourage the fantasy expression of these concerns and hence increase the subjects' anxiety. Since the experimental procedures were administered by persons other than the instructor, and since the attitude questionnaire was obviously quite different from the surprise test, there was little about the questionnaire to remind the subject of the test, while the task kept him occupied. Consequently, the attitude task would tend to delay the subject's fantasy exploration of his plight and hence hold down the development of anxiety.

To summarize, fantasy has the capacity either to increase or to decrease anxiety, depending on its timing in relation to the subject's concerns and incentives.

Aggression and Experimenter-Produced Films

It is apparent from the previous discussion that "vicarious fantasy" in the form of films, television, reading, etc., is quite different psychologically from subject-produced fantasy such as daydreams or TAT stories. The content of external media is fixed independently of the viewer's state, there is no possibility that the content can drift or cycle in accordance with the subject's inner processes, and, indeed, the role of viewer requires continued absorption in external stimuli.

The stimulus effects of films on fantasy are considered in Chapter 12. However, a considerable body of evidence has grown concerning the effect of viewing violent film sequences on the viewer's subsequent overt aggression. Since the results appear to be of only peripheral interest to a theory of fantasy proper, they will only be summarized here. More extensive discussions are available elsewhere (Berkowitz, 1962, 1964).

The preponderance of evidence, assembled in largest part by Berkowitz and his students, suggests that under certain conditions viewing violent films increases rather than reduces subjects' subsequent tendency to aggress. The conditions are that (a) the subject has first been angered, (b) the filmed violence seemed justified, and (c) the subject has available to him a target person whom he associates with the instigator of his anger. There may also be rare circumstances in which filmed violence reduces the tendency of angry subjects to aggress overtly (e.g., Feshbach, 1961). Although the necessary conditions are still uncertain, there is some suggestion (Berkowitz, 1960, 1962) that they may entail making subjects feel guilty about aggression through excessive violence.

In general, then, the effect of viewing violent films after insult is the opposite of spontaneously daydreaming. Violent films lack the structural properties of subject-produced fantasy and act instead to maintain or enhance tendencies to aggress. It is possible that films designed to mimic spontaneous fantasy structurally would have a similar effect of reducing aggressive tendencies, but such a possibility remains to be investigated.

TAT SCORES AS MEASURES OF MOTIVES

If the above analyses of motivational effects on fantasy are correct thus far, fantasy reflects current concerns which occur during incentive-oriented sequences of instrumental activity. The value of a particular incentive is in turn determined by anticipated states of drive. The statement that fantasy reflects current concerns should not be interpreted mechanistically. The case appears to be that current concerns potentiate corresponding content in fantasy, but there normally seem to be relatively rapid shifts in fantasy content, so that for practical purposes the relationship between a current concern and corresponding content in fantasy at a particular moment is probabilistic. In this restricted sense motivation influences the content of fantasy.

Although the present formulation aspires to a theory of fantasy in general, the stark fact is that most of the evidence on which it is based was obtained from TAT stories. Consequently, by the same chain of inference and in the same way, motivation influences the content of TAT stories.

It is important, however, to examine carefully just what sort of influence this is. The TAT was originally devised to study personalities; that is, to describe subjects' relatively enduring dispositions. Since its invention, the TAT has served most commonly as a diagnostic instrument to provide evidence concerning patients' functioning outside the context of the testing situation. The diagnostic and descriptive uses of the TAT assume a kind of motivational influence that is quite different from the one depicted here. It is the difference between a measure of an enduring disposition on the one hand and a probabilistic effect of a particular current concern on the other. In order to examine the TAT's claim to validity as a measure of motivation, it is necessary first to examine the properties of the instrument more closely and second to review the implications of the previous formulations of motivational effects on fantasy.

The TAT

Physically, the original TAT cards depict "classical human situations," that is, reasonably well defined classes of human experiences; and the many pictures that have been constructed subsequently were generally also designed to elicit reactions to well-defined classes of stimuli. TAT pictures are typically ambiguous only in a limited sense. Subjects can reach a high degree of consensus as to the numbers and approximate ages and sex of the characters depicted. The chief source of ambiguity for most of the pictures is thus the subject's ignorance regarding the context of the depicted situation: what is the relationship of the characters to one another, what has gone before, what feelings and thoughts underlie the expressions and actions frozen in the picture, how will the action end? Even in these regards the pictures considerably limit speculation. Some are clearly pastoral outdoor scenes, others are clearly indoor scenes, and so on.

The subject is asked to make up a complete, dramatic story about each picture. Since he must draw upon his internal resources to flesh out the insufficiency of cues provided by the picture, he must bring something of himself to the task of composing his story. That is, he must provide his "apperceptions" of the cues he perceives in order to give them full meaning. However, much of the apperceptive material is culturally prescribed, or, more accurately, the culture prescribes a certain range of material or set of acceptable alternatives from which the subject must choose. In a sense, the subject who writes a TAT story reveals something about his particular cognitive map of his society. Henry (1956) has pointed out that TAT pictures elicit certain modal story elements, and that the story material of interest for purposes of describing individuals is the set of idiosyncratic variations of a subject's stories around the culturally modal ones.

Administrations of the TAT or the TAT-like picture sets may require stories to one picture or to many, 20 being the number in the original Murray TAT. The Murray TAT attempted to sample a wide range of situations, but some special-purpose picture sets attempt to "pull" only a single kind of theme. The wider the range, clearly, the greater the sampling of the subject's apperceptive repertory and the better the chance that important concerns will emerge; but if the examiner obtains wide range at the cost of assessing a particular concern with only one picture, the validity and reliability of the method are bound to suffer on other, psychometric grounds.

The Subject

Written under such an elaborate set of constraints, the TAT story is obviously a different kind of product from spontaneous fantasy (Chapter 4). Nevertheless, it is true that the subject must bring to each story a considerable amount of specific content. He must at least choose among culturally implied alternatives. Whatever content he selects must have been more accessible to him than other possible content, must in other words have been better potentiated, and the evidence suggests that some of the potentiating factors can be summed up in the concept of current concerns.

At the moment of testing, however, normal subjects will be under the influence of several current concerns. The concerns are likely to vary in intensity but ordinarily none of them will be potent enough to preempt all thought. Presumably the effect of a particular current concern will be determined by its interaction with the picture cues. Concerns that seem inappropriate for a particular picture are unlikely to become conscious at decision time. Thus, the varied cues of the usual picture set may be expected to elicit many different kinds of fantasy themes as they interact with a subject's varied set of current concerns. Consequently, the TAT is unlikely to yield thematically consistent stories from one picture to the next.

Because current concerns depend on current goals or incentives, and because these fluctuate greatly in identity and intensity from one occasion to another, it is also unlikely that TAT administrations can yield stories that are thematically stable from one occasion to the next.

To sum up, TAT stories may reflect current concerns—concerns with incentives which the subject is actively pursuing—if the picture cues and the nature of the current concern are compatible. However, the internal consistency of scores based on more than one story and the stability of scores on more than one occasion are likely to be weak. In short the present formulation leads one to expect low reliability of TAT scores, an expectation amply supported by the evidence (Klinger, 1966, 1968). Furthermore, TAT scores cannot provide direct evidence concerning subjects' enduring motivational dispositions. To be sure, individuals' lives are not completely chaotic but are more or less ordered and continuous over time. Therefore one would expect that subjects who reveal certain current concerns at one point in time are more likely than chance to harbor a thematically similar concern again at a later point. One would therefore expect a positive correlation between TAT scores on particular occasions and subjects' enduring patterns of goal-seeking. Nevertheless, for all of the reasons indicated the correlation is likely to be weak, certainly too weak for effectively and dependably predicting individual behavior. Here, too, the present formulation agrees with the evidence, as experience with the highly researched *n* Ach score suggests (Klinger, 1966; Klinger and McNelly, 1969).

This is not to deny that the TAT has its uses. Stories composed from well-designed picture sets reflect the kinds of experimental manipulations reviewed earlier in this chapter. The thematic inconsistency among TAT stories limits the power of the technique, but since there are few efficient ways to assess the content characteristics of any kind of fantasy, TAT-like techniques may remain an indispensable tool in research on fantasy.

The clinical use of the TAT can perhaps be improved for diagnostic purposes if the limitations of the instrument are fully recognized. Systems might be developed for taking account of the interactions between picture cues and current concerns instead of simply adding up scores across heterogeneous pictures, and the picture sets might themselves be improved so as to sharpen the quest for particular kinds of information. Furthermore, it is possible to extract information about the subject's language and cognitive characteristics, much as one might with nonfantasy tasks that require subjects to speak or write extensively. However, the present formulation indicates that for purposes of measuring motivation TAT methods are inherently limited to illuminating the patient's current states; thus the desirability of improving TAT methods to obtain such information must be weighed against the costs, the limitations, and the availability of alternative methods.

CONCLUSIONS

The least cumbersome interpretation of the evidence reviewed in the present chapter can be summarized as follows:

1. Drives have little influence on fantasy except insofar as they enhance or diminish the value of incentives.

2. Unsettling events influence subsequent fantasy because these events are relevant to incentives that still lie in the future and mobilize new current concerns.

3. Fantasy is incapable of reducing drives as such; but because of its content-cycling character, fantasy can prevent or reverse the build-up of anger and can diminish anticipatory anxiety about unavoidable pain better than activities that continually cue off anger and anxiety.

4. TAT scores measure motives in the sense that they probabilistically reflect current concerns but not in the sense that they measure enduring motivational dispositions. The cyclical, drifting nature of fantasy limits the reliability of TAT methods.

CHAPTER 11

Fantasy and Overt Behavior

One of the questions of greatest interest in the field of fantasy concerns the reciprocal effects of fantasy and overt behavior. The previous three chapters deal with questions concerning the effects of instrumental response sequences on the thematic content of fantasy, and Chapter 7 touches on the effects of fantasy on creativity. However, there are other kinds of questions, which concern the relationship between an individual's typical pattern of fantasy—its frequency, form, and content—and his typical pattern of overt behavior. This class of questions is more macroscopic than those considered previously, for it deals not with moment-to-moment or segment-to-segment relationships, but with interrelationships among enduring individual dispositions. Furthermore, it has been of greatest interest not to students of fantasy as such but to investigators of motivation, personality, and psychodiagnosis. A great many such studies have been published during the past thirty years, especially during the 1950's, but the basic questions remain substantially unanswered.

The focus of the present book is on fantasy. The large volume of research that attempts to link fantasy patterns to patterns of overt behavior has shed relatively little light on the nature of fantasy itself. Since much of the evidence accumulated about the TAT is uninterpretable or of peripheral interest for purposes of developing a theory of fantasy, no attempt is made here to review the TAT area comprehensively. Much of the TAT literature concerns the validity of the TAT as a test, and a significant portion investigates gross psychodiagnostic relationships or other correlational evidence which is inapplicable to our present purposes. Competent general reviews of research on the TAT already exist, ranging from an extensive "interpretive lexicon for clinician and investigator" (Lindzey, Bradford, Tejessy, and Davids, 1959) to critical reviews and summaries (Murstein, 1963b; Rosenwald, 1968; Zubin, Eron, and Schumer, 1965). There is also a valuable symposium on general issues in the field (Kagan and Lesser, 1961). The most extensive programs of research have been directed at TAT achievement fantasy, which, with occasional offshoots into affiliative

316

and power fantasy, are reviewed extensively elsewhere (Atkinson, 1964; Atkinson and Feather, 1966; Birney, 1968; DeCharms, 1968; Heckhausen, 1967, 1968; Klinger, 1966; Klinger and McNelly, 1969). That portion of the latter literature which contributes to a theory of fantasy has already been discussed in previous chapters.

The extensive TAT literature has spawned at least one major issue which seems sufficiently germane to a theory of fantasy to warrant detailed attention. Sometimes called the "direct versus substitutive expression" controversy, it began as a debate over whether TAT stories reflect subjects' overt behavioral traits directly or whether they reflect those tendencies which subjects keep from expressing overtly. The controversy will form the topic of the following section.

Outside of the TAT literature, another vein of research has focused on the differences among people who report that they daydream with varying frequencies. The work has been amply described by Singer (1966) who, with his colleagues and students, is responsible for much of the research. The results will be summarized in a final section.

DIRECT VERSUS SUBSTITUTIVE EXPRESSION OF BEHAVIOR TENDENCIES IN TAT STORIES

A naive behavior theory can regard fantasy as a form of covert behavior consisting of learned habits of response. The covert responses are vestiges or symbolic representations of corresponding overt responses and obey the same laws, motivational and otherwise. In this conception a person's fantasies ought to resemble his overt behavior in its typical content. Whether the theory is naive or not, we have seen that in its most general terms it is similar to the general outlines of the theory propounded here, and the data appear to support it. The notion that fantasy expresses the same tendencies that a person expresses overtly is the "direct-expression" theory of fantasy.

This simple conception stands in contrast to the psychoanalytic theory, which challenged behavior theory in this respect as in so many others. In psychoanalytic terms, behavioral tendencies that can characteristically be expressed freely in behavior are precisely those which do *not* appear in fantasy, except perhaps as a disguise of the real, underlying tendencies— the "latent content"—of fantasy. When the satisfaction of needs is blocked, either because of physical obstacles or because of psychological conflicts, the needs are expressed in fantasy in the form of imaginary wish-fulfillments. Thus, fantasy forms an "alternative channel" to overt behavior for the expression of needs. Fantasy is a substitute for action. This, then, is the "substitutive-expression" theory of fantasy.

At first, behavior theorists met the challenge by accepting the psychoanalytic data and translating the psychoanalytic view into more acceptable, behaviorist language (e.g., Dollard and Miller, 1950). Furthermore, Miller's analysis of conflict permitted a behaviorist equivalent of the substitute-expression theory. Briefly, it is this. When an organism desires something, it is the more attracted to objects the more they resemble the actual incentive the organism seeks. Similarly, when an organism fears something, it fears objects according to how much they resemble what it is that the organism actually seeks to avoid. Changes in attractiveness or threat according to resemblance of something to something else are called "approach gradients" in the case of attraction and "avoidance gradients" in the case of avoidance. One of the key features of Miller's analysis is that avoidance gradients are steeper than approach gradients; that is, under certain circumstances, when an organism is both attracted and repelled by the same object, the two gradients intersect, with the result that the organism is more repelled than attracted to objects most like the actual goal object, but is more attracted than repelled by objects a little like the goal object (Figure 2). For instance a man who becomes overwhelmed by anxiety in the embrace of a lover may be greatly attracted by pornographic pictures or by the lingerie counter of a department store. Shifting one's behavioral focus away from a basic incentive to a less frightening but also less rewarding substitute is called displacement.

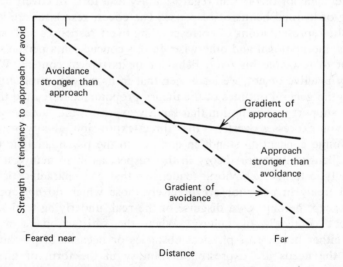

Figure 2. A graphic representation of conflict. The organism is moved to avoid objects that lie to the left of the intersection of the gradients, and is moved to approach those that lie to the right of the intersection. (From Miller, 1944, p. 434)

The measurement of drive and conflict in humans

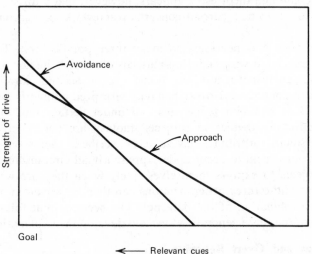

Figure 3. Conflict represented as the interaction of approach and avoidance drives along a stimulus dimension. The model is used for the measurement of conflict with specially constructed projective techniques. (From Epstein, 1962, p. 139)

This analysis can readily be applied to fantasy. Since fantasy has only some of the stimulus properties of actual events, a person can displace his wish for a feared real gratification to a safer, fantasy version. Thus, a person can safely express in fantasy those wishes that he cannot express overtly because he is afraid. This analysis has also been applied by Epstein (1962) to TAT fantasy to explain differences in the kinds of stories written to different TAT pictures (Figure 3). Thus a subject frightened by aggression may express greater hostility to a picture apparently remotely relevant to aggression than to a picture of violence.

Taking considerations of conflict and generalization gradients into account, then, behavior theory has been extended to agree with the substitutive-expression theory that fantasy may reflect tendencies whose overt expression is blocked by approach-avoidance conflicts. Additionally, the behavior theorist can continue to make the argument, contrary to the psychoanalytic view, that unblocked tendencies may also color fantasy. This combined view actually accords with that of Murray (1943), who originated the TAT.

The controversy between adherents to direct expression and partisans of substitutive expression has generated considerable data, whose complexity has failed to provide unequivocal support to either side and has spawned a number of combined theories. It appears, however, that a direct-expression theory, reworked to fit a current-concerns framework, can accomodate the data.

To begin with it is necessary to make three points. First, TAT scores are poorly correlated with enduring patterns of overt behavior in any case, as the earlier analysis suggests we should expect. Second, correlations between fantasy content and overt behavior are predominantly positive for certain kinds of behavior tendencies and under certain kinds of circumstances. Third, the themes in subjects' fantasy are correlated positively with the personality attributes that subjects ascribe to themselves. The positive correlations seem to occur under apparently all circumstances that encourage subjects to express themselves freely when they are writing their TAT stories. These three generalizations can then be woven into an incentive-related explanation of the data net. The sections that follow explore the validity of the three generalizations and develop the explanation.

TAT Stories and Overt Behavior

There are many kinds of overt behavior, and the way in which fantasy content relates to overt behavioral content depends to some degree on the kind of behavior in question. However, the relationships are relatively weak in the case of all of the following kinds of behavior.

Achievement fantasy has been found postitively correlated with subjects' characteristic patterns of actual achievement in about half of the studies that have been reported (Klinger, 1966). The relationship is more consistent with subjects below college age than with college students. The mass of evidence indicates that subjects who engage in much achievement fantasy begin to do so after they have already begun to achieve in actuality (Skolnick, 1966). That is, achievement fantasy changes to reflect an individual's life circumstances, rather than reflecting long-term motivational dispositions which in turn alter life circumstances. There is reason to believe that a major determinant of how much a person fantasies about achievement is his current social role which is tied to his current social status (Klinger and McNelly, 1969). Since a person's role prescribes many of his day-to-day concerns, such a conclusion is entirely consistent with the present theory. Social status is probably the underlying social factor which is responsible for much of the relationship between TAT achievement fantasy and performance. Subjects who are expected to do well become concerned with achievement and consequently fantasy about it.

There are, however, many factors which weaken the relationship between achievement fantasy and performance. When college populations are relatively homogeneous socially, status variables differentiate less among students and weaken relationships between performance and fantasy. Furthermore, students strive after academic grades for many reasons besides the joy of accomplishment, such as obedience to authority, dependency, fear of failure, economic gain, and evading military conscription. Some of these incentives may increase students' achievement fantasy as well as forcing students to maintain at least a minimum level of academic performance, but the level of concern and the level of performance necessary to allay the concern vary widely with the particular goal, the student's ability, his other commitments, etc. The upshot is that the relationship between achievement fantasy and performance is so weak as to be practically negligible, even when one takes careful account of the differences among instructors and classrooms (McKeachie et al., 1968).

Subjects who fantasy frequently about achievement are distinguished in some other behavioral respects as well as performance; for example, they are more inclined than others to seek moderately difficult achievement challenges (e.g., Atkinson, 1964). In this behavior as in performance, subjects appear to reflect the consequences of their social status (Klinger and McNelly, 1969). One interpretation is that these subjects simply gain greater intrinsic satisfaction from meeting an honest challenge. However, when they think they are unobserved they are more likely to falsify their scores (Mischel and Gilligan, 1964)—that is, to cheat. Thus there is evidence that they are extremely concerned with appearances, others' assessment of their performance, as well as with accomplishment for its own sake. They behave as if they are deeply concerned to preserve their social status with respect to achievement.

Subjects whose TAT stories are marked by fear of failure or hostile press—whose fantasied achievement strivings are unhappy experiences and who are often victims of malign circumstances—tend in actuality to be more protective of their pride, to undergo fewer risks of embarrassment and failure (Birney, Burdick, and Teevan, 1969). They tend to seek safety in the form of predictably manageable tasks, diffused responsibility, and extenuating circumstances. Here, again, the relationships are not overwhelming but predominantly positive.

All in all, then, granting the weakness of the relationships, achievement-related fantasy appears to obey a direct-expression law. Of course, achievement is a rather special kind of overt behavior, entailing highly deliberate activity and a great deal of conscious strategy and control. Does the generalization extend to more emotionally toned behavior?

In a number of respects the answer appears to be affirmative; for instance, the TAT fantasies and overt stress reactions of hospitalized children correspond closely in the relative prominence of aggression, dependency, and anxiety, and the foci of their fears in fantasy (such as separation, physicians, injections, etc.) also tend to precipitate their overt stress reactions (Barton, 1964). College students who write relatively sexual TAT stories report that they normally experience a high frequency of orgasms (Epstein and Smith, 1957; Leiman & Epstein, 1961).

A number of relatively stable kinds of interpersonal behavior patterns are also related to corresponding themes in subjects' TAT stories. Male student politicians and office-holders produce more themes in which story characters strive for social influence and status (Skolnick, 1966; Veroff, 1957; Winter, 1968). Affiliative fantasy may be related to needs and problems concerning social support, for college students who have been rejected by fraternities tell more affiliative TAT stories than students who have been pledged (Shipley and Veroff, 1952); and, although the relationships are very weak, so do male adolescents who are rated by others as needing social ties, lacking self-sufficiency, and exhibiting dependency (Skolnick, 1966). Subjects whose story characters engage in dependent activity have been rated clinically as conflicted about dependency (Fitzgerald, 1958) and are more likely than others to conform to group opinions (Kagan and Mussen, 1956). The TAT stories of homosexual male subjects differ from those of heterosexuals in containing more confused or unstable gender identity and more negative attitudes toward women and heterosexual relationships (Lindzey, Tejessy, and Zamansky, 1958).

So far, then, the direct-expression view receives support from similarities between TAT stories and a wide variety of behavioral modes. One important kind of interpersonal behavior remains to be considered: aggression. Here the picture seems ostensibly different. Although a number of studies have found generally positive correlations between TAT and overt aggression (James and Mosher, 1967; Kagan, 1956; Lesser, 1958; Mussen and Naylor, 1954; Purcell, 1956; Stone, 1956), a number of others have not (Brenner, 1963; Coleman, 1967; Heymann, 1955; Jensen, 1957; Lasky, 1961; Lindzey and Tejessy, 1956; Murstein, 1965, 1968; Skolnick, 1966). (Classifying Skolnick's work here may be disputed. Of 612 aggression-related correlation coefficients reported, 42 were significant beyond the .05 level. The variables most relevant to overt personal aggression were mostly uncorrelated with TAT aggression. Those variables most consistently correlated with TAT aggression were observer's "drive ratings" which were based on covert indications of aggression and clinical inference as well as on overt indications.) In two groups TAT aggression has been found inversely associated with overt aggression (Lesser, 1957, 1959; Schaefer and Norman, 1967).

The factor that seems to moderate the relationship, determining whether fantasy aggression is postively or negatively related to overt aggression, is the degree of social support for aggression. Lower-class culture is more accepting of direct personal aggression than is middle class culture, for instance. Society generally tolerates more direct personal aggression the younger the age group of the subject. Five of the six studies cited above which found direct correlations between fantasy and overt aggression drew their subjects from military groups (Purcell, 1956; Stone, 1956), from a deliberately chosen lower-class population (Mussen and Naylor, 1954), or from upper-lower-class (Lesser, 1958) or skilled-labor (Kagan, 1956) backgrounds. The last of these groups averaged less than eight years in age. Of the eight studies that found no relationship, four used college students, three used high school groups at least one of which was enrolled in a college preparatory sequence, and one used 10- and 13-year-old British boys an unspecified portion of whom were drawn from lower-middle class as well as lower-class origins. Lesser's (1957, 1959) results are particularly cogent against the background of these data. He divided his sample of prepubertal boys into one group whose mothers supported aggression and a second group whose mothers discouraged aggression. In the first group, the correlation between fantasy and overt aggression was positive; in the second group, it was negative.

The data thus appear to permit the generalization that when a kind of behavior pattern is supported by the surrounding society, it tends to be expressed in fantasy directly; whereas, if a kind of behavior pattern is punished by society, its opposite tends to be expressed in fantasy. The data reviewed above all pertain to aggression. However, Skolnick (1966) found that power-seeking by adult women, whom contemporary society often punishes for that kind of behavior, tends slightly to be inversely related to power themes in TAT stories. There is thus some basis for hope that the generalization holds true for a range of behavior broader than aggression alone.

Faced with a generalization of this kind, one may be tempted to imagine a kind of mechanistic, or perhaps hydraulic, process. Given that a person's aggression is punished, he represses his hostility, but the unsatisfied need to aggress manifests itself in hostile fantasies for reasons beyond his conscious understanding. There are, however, two reasons for rejecting such an interpretation. First of all, such subjects' TAT stories contain not only the aggression but also their awareness that aggression begets punishment or otherwise ought to be inhibited. Second, people with hostile fantasies tend to regard themselves as genuinely hostile, and probably they inhibit their aggression for the at least partly conscious reason that they wish to avoid the unpleasantness engendered by it.

With respect to punishment, subjects whose TAT stories contain elements in which characters sustain physical or psychological injury as a result of aggressing are less likely than others to aggress overtly. TAT aggression is in some groups a poor predictor of overt aggression, as we have seen; but when the TAT aggression score is combined with a score that reflects voluntary inhibition of aggression by story characters or reflects discomfort suffered as a result of aggression (e.g., by subtracting the TAT inhibition score from or dividing it into the TAT aggression score) the prediction of overt aggression from TAT content is markedly improved (Lesser, 1958; McCasland, 1961). Subjects who are given to overt aggression are more likely than nonaggressors to omit punishment for aggression in TAT stories, particularly internal self-punishments such as remorse, self-blame, or loss of loved ones (Jensen, 1957; Purcell, 1956). Subjects who regard themselves as hostile but whose acquaintances regard them as friendly tell TAT stories which portray particularly prominent internal punishments for aggression (Murstein, 1968).

Clearly, then, frustrated aggression manifests itself in TAT fantasy as something other than unadorned wishfulfillment. The subject recognizes the ill consequences of aggression in fantasy, and apparently also utilizes this information in inhibiting his overt aggression. The pattern of results suggests the intervention of a conscious, deliberate process. The extent to which subjects recognize the significance of their hostile fantasies and impulses is indicated by their readiness to incorporate the hostility into their self-concepts.

TAT Stories and Self-Concepts

Early analysts of TAT stories often employed the "hero assumption" that the heroes of the stories (i.e., the central characters) carry the burden of conveying the characteristics of the story-teller, whereas the nonhero characters are far less revealing. The hero assumption received support from evidence obtained by Lindzey and Kalnins (1958) that subjects identify heroes as resembling themselves, or in some cases as typifying the opposite of themselves, more than nonheroes, whereas nonheroes are more likely to represent stereotyped figures unrelated to the subjects' self-concepts.

A number of investigators have reported positive correlations between subjects' TAT stories and their self-descriptions. Subjects who claim to dislike sexual activity or disapprove of it tell fewer sexual TAT stories (Leiman and Epstein, 1961). The family relationships which subjects describe in TAT stories resemble their own family relationships as the subjects perceive them (Calogeras, 1957). Subjects who write achievement-flavored stories describe a greater discrepancy between the kind of achievement traits they aspire to and those they believe they have attained.

By and large, subjects who write about aggression in TAT stories also describe themselves as relatively more hostile than other subjects do (Kaplan, 1967; Lindzey and Tejessey, 1956; Murstein, 1965, 1968; Rosenbaum and Stanners, 1961; Saltz and Epstein, 1963). There are some negative results reported by Lasky (1961), who scored both TAT stories and self-reported daydream samples, and by Brenner (1963), whose TAT "hostility" scores were, however, an amalgam of hostility, defensiveness, and other elements extraneous to hostility as such.

The positive results were occasionally reported with qualifications. Thus, when Saltz and Epstein (1963) inspected the stories of subjects who reject aggression as a mode of social response they found an *inverse* relationship between injury to nonheroes ("hostility") and hostile self-reports. It should be noted that their self-report scale for hostility largely asked about hostile spontaneous fantasy, often in response to instigations. Perhaps the relatively rare subject who rejects aggressive values but responds to provocation with angry daydreams avoids hostile confrontations so adamantly that he rarely entertains a hostile current concern and therefore writes relatively nonhostile TAT stories.

There are also method-related qualifications. Kaplan (1967) and James and Mosher (1967) obtained positive relationships between TAT and self-reported hostility only with those of their TAT pictures that were most relevant to aggression, while Saltz and Epstein (1963) obtained the result with those of their pictures that were least relevant to aggression. Rosenbaum and Stanners (1961) obtained their result only after arousing subjects to anger. Different investigators used somewhat different subject populations and methods. There is a clear need for parametric investigations to discover more precisely the conditions under which the relationship holds.

Meanwhile, the persistence of positive relationships across a number of additional investigations imparts some confidence in the conclusion that hostile TAT fantasies tend to be produced by subjects who regard themselves as hostile.

Investigators have obtained some interesting relationships involving anti-aggressive factors. Subjects who claim to reject aggression as a mode of social response write more stories in which heroes are injured, which Saltz and Epstein interpret as projected "guilt," than do subjects who are more accepting of aggression. They also write fewer aggressive stories (James and Mosher, 1967) and fewer hostile stories, that is, those in which nonheroes are injured (Saltz and Epstein, 1963). However, subjects who describe themselves as hostile experience greater remorse and guilt ("conflict") by their own account than do less hostile subjects (Saltz and Epstein, 1963) and their TAT stories contain more internal punishments of the hero (Murstein, 1968). Thus, both acceptance or rejection of aggression and the subject's anticipated consequences of aggression seem to be represented in TAT fantasy directly.

It may be that subjects base their self-concepts partly on their self-knowledge of their past inner experience. Leary (1956) asked subjects to describe themselves before and after a six-month interval on two dimensions, love-hate and dominance-submission. On the first occasion they also wrote TAT stories that were scored on the same dimensions. Some subjects produced large discrepancies between their TAT scores and their first self-descriptions. Six months later, their new self-descriptions tended to have changed in the direction of the initial TAT scores, and the larger the initial discrepancy, the greater the change.

Across a number of different kinds of behavior and emotional response, then, TAT fantasy and subjects' concepts of themselves are in agreement. As Lindzey and Tejessy (1956) stated about their data, "These findings suggest rather strongly that the scores we had derived painstakingly from the TAT protocols represent rather accurately the information we could have secured from the subjects themselves by simply asking them to appraise their own behavior. [p. 573]."

A Possible Resolution of the Direct Versus Substitutive Expression Controversy

The thrust of the TAT evidence reviewed above can be summarized as follows:

1. All relationships between TAT scores and overt behavior tend to be weak.

2. If a kind of activity is generally accepted by society, its occurrence in subjects' overt behavior is positively correlated with its occurrence in their TAT stories.

3. If a kind of activity is socially disapproved, its occurrence in subjects' overt behavior is *inversely* correlated with its expression in their TAT stories. Particularly, when aggression is socially disapproved subjects who are overtly least aggressive tell the most aggressive TAT stories.

4. Subjects who inhibit overt aggression are more likely than others to tell TAT stories that portray the ill consequences of aggression, especially internal self-punishments and loss of love.

5. The occurrence of a certain kind of behavior in TAT stories is positively correlated with subjects' descriptions of themselves as harboring the corresponding tendencies. Particularly, subjects who tell hostile TAT stories are likely to describe themselves as hostile.

All of these points except the third are plainly consistent with a direct-expression approach to TAT stories and are consistent with the general theoretical orientation of this book. The snag appears to reside in the third point. How does one explain by direct-expression theory that under some circumstances overtly nonaggressive subjects tell more aggressive TAT stories than do overtly aggressive subjects?

The explanation requires recognizing some distinctions.

1. *Overt behavior is the end result of a decision process which includes a number of terms, prominent among which is the expected pay-off of each alternative behavior.* It is unnecessary to suppose that subjects who tell hostile stories but are overtly unaggressive repress or deny their hostility in action. Indeed, the evidence indicates that subjects are generally quite aware of their hostile impulses. However, they are also aware of their fears and apprehensions and may consequently suppress overt aggression even while seething with anger.

2. *There are at least two different ways to be nonaggressive.* First, one may be nonaggressive because aggressive responses have seldom worked to obtain a goal and because other, nonaggressive responses have proved generally effective. With instrumental aggressive responses largely extinguished and effective nonaggressive responses well instated, the person can be usually nonaggressive and usually nonhostile without much conflict. Aggression is simply low on his hierarchy of response to social problems. A second way of being nonaggressive is quite different, however. The person has retained strong aggressive tendencies for a variety of possible reasons. Perhaps his aggressive responses have been intermittently reinforced. Perhaps he has learned few other responses to interpersonal problems that are reliably effective, or perhaps the people around him are relatively insensitive to all but aggressive acts. However, aggression is frequently also punished in this individual's case, with the result that he often holds his aggressive tendencies in check. Such an individual should regard himself as hostile and frequently tell hostile TAT stories, but his stories should also contain many avoidant and self-punitive elements and his overt actions should seem normally unaggressive, despite considerable conscious conflict.

3. *The fact that cultural norms or social disapproval are uniform for a subculture does not result in necessarily uniform experiences for different subjects.* On the contrary, subjects are likely to be punished for infractions of rules in some relationship to their tendency to disobey, which may vary. Furthermore, different agents of socialization mete out different mixtures of rewards and punishments and thereby greatly vary the incentive properties of obeying or infringing the same social norms.

These considerations may now be applied to the case of aggression in social settings that disapprove of it. Presumably people are on the average less aggressive in these circumstances than in settings which support aggression (Lesser, 1952). Some subjects will generally be slow to anger and aggress because they have been taught effective, nonaggressive responses for dealing with potentially frustrating situations and because the nonaggressive responses are generally reinforced. Such subjects would rarely be in the midst of a hostile current concern and hence would express little hostility in their TAT stories. However, when they are provoked and when a situation exhausts their nonaggressive repertory, they can be expected to aggress. Compared to some other subjects, they may even aggress overtly more often.

Consider now the other subjects. They have perhaps not been taught very effective nonaggressive responses; or perhaps their nonaggressive responses were often unheeded in their training environment whereas angry outbursts gained attention. These subjects, frequently frustrated and driven to aggression, perhaps experienced greater punishment for aggression than the more fortunate, socially more versatile subjects. In a sense they experienced in their lifetime more trials of passive-avoidance training to withhold hostile responses. Thus, these subjects learn both the positive and aversive consequences of aggression. Aggression remains high on their response hierarchy, but it is normally overshadowed by the apprehension of punishment, especially conditioned feelings of remorse, guilt, or shame. Their apprehension is great not only relative to their aggressive tendencies but also relative to the apprehension experienced by the less hostile and therefore less often punished subjects. Hence, their record of overt behavior may include even less overt aggression than the records of the less hostile subjects, but their frequent hostile current concerns and their apprehensions over their aggression both find direct expression in their TAT stories. To state this in still another way, some subjects respond to frustrating social situations with a complex of aggressive subgoals and anxieties that stud their TAT protocols but not their social actions; whereas other subjects respond to similar situations with predominantly nonaggressive subgoals and actions, which leave their TAT protocols largely free of hostility, but occasionally they act aggressively without much conflict or apprehension.

When one combines subjects who rarely tell hostile TAT stories but sometimes aggress overtly with subjects who tell many hostile stories but rarely aggress, the result is an inverse correlation between TAT hostility and overt aggression. This is the kind of result that undergirds the substitutive-expression theory of fantasy; but as the above analysis suggests, fantasy is not a "substitute" for overt action in any psychological sense. Rather, in environments that punish aggression, their inverse relationship arises from the same normal operation of incentives and concerns that has been described for the general case in which fantasy and overt behavior are correlated loosely but directly.

This formulation assumes some properties of socializing environments. It assumes, for instance, that subcultures which discourage aggression have a certain tolerance level for it, a certain threshold for permissible aggression. When a child's aggression exceeds the threshold level, he brings punishment down on his head. The more attractive aggression seems, the more often the child is likely to aggress and be punished. Perhaps the threshold drops or rises if a child repeats the infraction an abnormal number of times. In any case the condition which brings about the severest or most frequent punishment is the child's tendency to commit aggression, and that seems likely to depend in turn on the reinforcement of aggression, the unavailability of alternative responses, the frustratingness of other persons with whom the child must interact, and possibly innate constitutional variables. These assumptions provide a set of testable hypotheses by which the validity of the formulation may be evaluated in the future.

Although the present theory contains some novel features, it is still classifiable as essentially a "direct-expression" position. Whether or not this particular explanation of the "substitutive-expression" phenomenon turns out to be correct, the larger point is that all existing TAT data can at this stage of the science still be explained parsimoniously without invoking any special mechanisms, simply by applying the principles of fantasy that are elaborated in the previous chapters.

ATTENTION TO INTERNAL EVENTS: INDIVIDUAL DIFFERENCES

Previous sections examine the relationships between preferences for certain kinds of overt behavior and certain kinds of thematic content in fantasy. There is another class of questions, however, that asks about the relationships between subjects' overt behavior and their disposition to engage in fantasy of any kind in preference to other kinds of thought or action. This seemingly straightforward set of questions actually presents some considerable complications. First of all, it can be said flatly that no information exists concerning individuals' tendency to engage in more or less fantasy activity. Information does exist, however, on some matters that may be related to this: first, the frequency with which people estimate that they have daydreams—generally meaning fantasies organized into sequences whose content is readily definable and consistent for a stretch of time—and second, the imaginativeness of projective fantasies, especially in response to Rorschach inkblots. Most of the research on these questions has been organized around studies of two variables, Rorschach human movement (M) and frequency scores obtained with the Singer-McCraven General Daydream Questionnaire (Singer and McCraven, 1961); it has been reviewed extensively by Singer (1960, 1966).

M is the number of times a subject responds to Rorschach inkblots by describing humans in motion: for example, "two people dancing." The Rorschach M score has been found correlated with a wide variety of theoretically relevant variables which suggest that it measures a preference for thought over action: less motor activity or stimulus-seeking when subjects are forced to wait (Singer and Herman, 1954; Singer and Spohn, 1954); incidence of EEG alpha rhythm, which tends to be disrupted by visual and problem-solving activity (Rabinovitch, Kennard, and Fister, 1955); ratings by observers that characterize high-M subjects as unusually thoughtful, introspective, and intellectual (Barron, 1955); lesser reliance on external stimuli in formulating verbal associations (Mann, 1956); preference for nonmotoric games over more active ones (Riess, 1957); the tendency not to overestimate the length of time during enforced idleness, which low-M subjects overestimate (Kurz, Cohen, and Starzynski, 1965); and, quite central to the argument, self-ratings on the Page Fantasy Scale, which is much like the General Daydream Questionnaire (Reiter, 1963). M has also been found correlated with self-control of emotional responses, but those interesting data largely fall outside the purview of the present analysis.

The General Daydream Questionnaire asks subjects "to indicate the frequency (on a six-point scale) with which they had experienced each of a series of approximately one hundred daydreams [Singer, 1966, p. 56]" such as "I plan how to increase my income in the next year," or "I have my own yacht and plan a cruise on the Eastern Seaboard." Unfortunately, the General Daydream Questionnaire produces data that are at least three large steps removed from its objective of measuring subjects' inclination to fantasy. First, since it measures only subjects' retrospective self-reports, it can only tap fantasies of which the subject took note and which he remembered. Second, since the subject must check the frequency of daydreams listed by the Questionnaire, it omits subjects' idiosyncratic daydreams and therefore measures frequency of remembering *common* daydreams. Since the standardization samples were unrepresentative of any specifiable population beyond that defined by the particular sampling procedures, the Questionnaire measures frequency of remembering daydreams common in socioculturally biased samples. Third, since the Questionnaire asks the subject to report generalizations about his patterns of daydreaming, the results also measure subjects' willingness and ability to report accurately.

In light of such limitations in the instrument—which, in fairness to the investigators, are extravagantly difficult to avoid—it is not surprising that

Structure and Functions of Fantasy: The Theory in Propositional Form

The decision to construct a theory of fantasy sprang from the need to break a vicious circle that led from a dearth of data to a poverty of theory and back to discouragement of programmatic data-gathering. To break the circle required a bootstrap operation: the synthesis of a theory from data that were often gathered to attain some other objective.

The theory can serve its purpose best if it is cast in a form conducive to deriving experimental hypotheses. The previous material is, however, organized in the form of a search—a search for the makings of a theory of fantasy. That form of organization has the value of permitting particular chapters to correspond to recognizable divisions of psychological investigation, and it has the value of retaining a record of the heuristic process, but it obscures somewhat the structure of the theory that has emerged.

This appendix is intended to accomplish two principal objectives, systematization and sketching of implications for future research and application. It is organized to present the theory in a somewhat reordered form and to make explicit some of the relationships among its parts. In order to accomplish its purposes most expeditiously, it presents the theory as a set of more or less concise propositions, each followed by a brief section summarizing the status of the proposition—its grounding in evidence, its logical relationships to other propositions, etc. The propositions are intended as a series of explicit assertions for empirical test, parametric specification, and logical reconstruction.

1. PROPOSITIONS REGARDING THE SEGMENTAL ORGANIZATION OF BEHAVIOR

1.1 *Sequences of behavior, including expressions of ideation, can be divided into segments in such a way that the homogeneity of thematic content within a segment is greater than its resemblance to the content of adjacent segments.*

Evidence for the proposition takes the form of demonstrating that such segmentation can be performed reliably, as reported by Barker and his colleagues with respect to childrens' behavior and in Chapter 4 with regard to protocols from subjects who are instructed to "think out loud."

Because projective techniques artificially restrict the flow of subjects' responses, they are poorly suited for studying the structure of free fantasy, even though they may provide valuable data concerning global thematic content.

1.2 *Segmentation may be identified at several levels of organization, such that it is often possible to identify segments within segments.*

The evidence is similar to that for Proposition 1.1.

1.3 *Segments of homogeneous content are functionally coherent.*

That is, segments identifiable by content analysis reflect aspects of actual behavioral organization, such that the reaction properties of organisms at the juncture between two segments are different from their reaction properties within the boundaries of a segment. Some evidence for the proposition as it relates to relatively low-order segments arises from psycholinguistic studies of "chunking" (Chapter 6). Casual observation also suggests that people respond differently to interruption at the end of a segment of content from the way they respond to interruption in the middle.

2. OPERANT AND RESPONDENT SEGMENTS

2.1 *Segments of activity may be classified into two broad groups which are here called "operant" and "respondent." Whereas operant segments are initiated ("emitted") volitionally, controlled by consequences, guided by feedback, and therefore proactive, respondent segments are initiated nonvolitionally, are not inherently dependent on feedback, are elicited by antecedent events, and are therefore reactive.*

With the partial exception of its volitional aspects, the distinction follows theory and practice in studies of classical conditioning and of course borrows its terminology from Skinner. The distinction also has some close parallels to the Freudian distinction between primary- and secondary-process thought. Although it may often be difficult to distinguish respondent from operant segments when these are passively recorded in verbal protocols, the proposition does suggest operations whereby the nature of a segment can be tested, for instance by such experimental interventions as manipulating feedback or antecedent conditions.

The feedback mentioned in the proposition refers to feedback concerning the consequences of the segment, such as how far it had advanced the subject toward a goal. This kind of feedback is irrelevant in determining the course of a respondent sequence but crucial to the course of an operant one. "Feedback" as used here is, however, not intended to refer to yet another process that seems likely to occur but must still be regarded as controversial: the control exerted over the unfolding of a single brief act by its "meaning-complex," "grammar plan," or "motor program," as for instance in the correct enunciation of a word or the production of a brief sentence. Such hierarchical control over emerging behavior may well entail a kind of intrasegmental feedback to make possible the execution of the intended brief act, but in that case it would seem to characterize respondent as well as operant segments.

Respondent segments include behavior whose content appears operant but is functionally respondent because of the circumstances in which it occurs; for instance, the mathematician who dreams of transposing matrices has produced a functionally respondent segment provided that the onset of the segment did not originate in an actual problem-solving sequence and that the following segment occurs independently of the success of the earlier segment in advancing a goal.

Conversely, an individual may undertake to simulate respondent processes for some specific purpose; for instance, he may construct a daydream to console himself during a depressed mood or to build up his confidence. Such sequences are functionally operant, at least at their outset, since their construction is guided by an intended end result and since they are subject to correction and modification in the pursuit of the objective.

2.2 *Just as operant segments may succeed one another in a "chain", in which the completion of each segment serves as the discriminative stimulus for the onset of the next, so respondent segments may also succeed one another in a chain, some event in one segment serving as an elicitor of the next respondent segment.*

There are conditioning data that support the proposition, as well as numerous suggestive instances in published dream and daydream protocols.

2.3 *Respondent segments are accompanied by little subjective sense of mental effort, less than most operant segments.*

Although the proposition reflects the consensus of introspectionists and clinicians who have commented on the matter, there seem to be no published systematic data to support or refute it.

2.4 *Fantasy, dreams, and early childhood play, as these are construed in common usage, consist predominantly of respondent segments.*

Chapters 1 and 2 provide working definitions of fantasy and dreams that exclude instrumental activities. The construction of a working definition was required at the outset in order to delimit the problem to be considered. In light of these definitions, however, Proposition 2.4 might appear tautological. It is saved from tautology in that it employs not the working definitions introduced earlier but rather the looser body of frequently implicit definitions in general use. The proposition thus constitutes an empirically testable assertion, that most of the components of what most people consider to be fantasy, dreams, and play are respondent rather than operant.

The evidence for the proposition is at present largely casual, but it derives support from observations of animal play and of children's play and imaginative activity.

2.5 *Psychological activity is substantially continuous throughout both waking and sleep. In the absence of operant activity and perceptual scanning, intermittently during predominantly operant sequences, and sometimes concurrently with integrated operant activity, mental activity consists of respondent sequences.*

It is logically impossible to test a proposition that mental activity never ceases during a lifetime, since a total hiatus in mental activity, strictly defined, entails also a hiatus in the capacity to experience or store a memory of it. It is necessary therefore to restrict the proposition to those interruptions of the experiential stream that are in principle somehow detectable. There appears, however, to have been general agreement among introspectionist psychologists that conscious awareness continues uninterrupted during waking, and studies of dreaming provide reasons to believe that mentation continues throughout sleep.

The principal consequence of assuming continuous psychological activity around the clock is that if all behavior can be divided into operant, scanning, and respondent segments, then the subsidence of nonrespondent activity is necessarily tantamount to the onset of respondent activity. Since operant segments probably feel more effortful and may be more fatiguing than at least some respondent activities such as fantasy or dreaming, it is attractive to consider respondent activity as constituting a kind of behavioral baseline, below which the level of activity cannot fall, and from which it departs in the execution of operant sequences.

2.6 *Respondent sequences are more often fractionated and are more readily abandoned than are operant sequences.*

Since respondent segments are directed at no goals and make little use of feedback, behavior during respondent sequences is more distractible and interruptable. The proposition gains support from observational studies of play in animals and young children, but the data are poorly systematized.

3. THE COMPOSITION OF SEGMENTS

3.1   *Ideation, including imagery, consists of efferent activity and consti-
       tutes a form of response process. As such, it possesses the attributes
       of other response phenomena.*

The proposition rests on evidence that even certain forms of perception involve efferent activity; that imagery is a constructive process, one that reconstructs certain cognized or discriminated aspects of sensory experiences; and that images and their behavioral indications, if one includes evidence from sensory preconditioning experiments, can be conditioned and extinguished in important respects like other kinds of behavior, and they exhibit the effects of stimulus discrimination and potentiation by motivational states. Insofar as this evidence demonstrates the response-like character of imagery and ideation, the components of fantasy also possess other properties of nonimaginal responses.

3.2   *Fantasy and dreams consist partly of imagery at least at most times.*

That appears to be the introspectionist consensus. The chief disagreement is whether "most times" should read "all times." The history of psychology suggests that pursuit of that controversy is scientifically unprofitable.

3.3   *The ideational facets of fantasy segments form parts of response
       complexes ("subselves") whose ramifications extend beyond the purely
       imaginal responses which register most clearly in consciousness to
       include affects, attitudes, and occasionally unconscious directive in-
       fluences.*

Whether or not imagery is continuously present in consciousness, imagery is clearly not all of what there is to fantasy. The Würzburg experiments on "set" determinants of thought processes and recent experiments on the determinants and correlates of achievement fantasy suggest that fantasies, like other thought, are directed and potentiated by factors that may be unconscious during some or all of the fantasy sequence. Furthermore, conscious facets of fantasy seem to form part of a state that also includes related affects, goals, and self-perceptions. Thus, the content of fantasy may be construed as an aspect of a person's momentary self-state. Since a person's self-states seem to vary, and since the states seem to have been organized prior to the situations that arouse them and are therefore probably relatively enduring properties of a personality, they have here been called "subselves." Subselves transcend segments in level of organization, in that the period during which a subself is regnant may encompass many more than one segment of fantasy. The subself construct is at this stage of the theory primarily descriptive rather than explanatory, and it is particularly incapable of explaining the organization of individual segments or the sequencing of segments within the period in which a single subself is regnant.

3.4   *At some levels of segmentation, fantasy segments are organized hierarchically, the particular constituents of a segment unfolding under the control of a "meaning-complex," which is an inarticulate but clearly structured response state whose formation must precede the segment.*

Several lines of evidence produced by psycholinguists suggest that linguistic units are already fully organized before the first word in the unit is spoken. The speaker seems to know in advance what he intends to say, and he can if necessary encode his intended meaning in numerous alternative verbal expressions. Early parts of his message are formed so as to accommodate what he will say later. If he is unable to think of a word which he needs to express himself, he gropes around in full awareness that he is unable to produce the word and rejects unsuitable substitutes despite his inability to produce the correct word. All of these evidences of hierarchical organization embarrass strictly associationist theories, although modern S-R versions have generated new concepts, some of them inherently nonassociationist, in order to counter the psycholinguistic assault.

Although most of the relevant theorizing has been performed to account for sentences and smaller linguistic units, the principle of hierarchic organization would seem to apply equally well at the level of the paragraph and at even more complex levels. Since much fantasy takes verbal forms, it seems reasonable to suppose that the principle of hierarchic organization applies also to at least some levels of the organization of fantasy. Accordingly, fantasy appears not to obey the classical laws of association within segments generally.

The principle of hierarchic organization of segments requires logically that prior to each segment's unfolding, some response event or state occur which contains the plan for the structure and meaning content of the segment and which can control the unfolding process. That is what is here called a "meaning-complex." It is inarticulate in the sense that it can recruit alternative verbal expressions but does not itself contain the word responses themselves, as becomes evident in the instance of being unable to retrieve the right word to express an intended meaning. In fantasy, which often contains at most a highly vestigial representation of speech, meaning can be experienced without requiring all of the "right" words to occur.

The phrase "at some levels of segmentation" is deliberately ambiguous. Operationally, segments are now defined as shifts in content, and those shifts can occur at different levels of detail. A subject who ruminates for 20 minutes about his relationship with his girl-friend has spent 20 minutes on a girl-friend segment, but it is unlikely that the entire 20-minute sequence was hierarchically preorganized at the outset. On the other hand, if after reviewing her personality attributes he shifts to the question of her appearance and engages in a one-sentence "sub-subroutine" segment of "She's prettier than Roberta," it is entirely likely that this small segment was hierarchically preorganized at the outset. What is needed in order to specify "some levels" more closely is a functional taxonomy for segments derived from content analysis, but the taxonomy does not yet exist and neither does the necessary data base.

3.5 *At some level of segmental organization, all segments of fantasy are integrated response sequences.*

Chapter 6 undertakes a reanalysis of the concept of response integration, emerging with a set of criteria for distinguishing integrated response sequences. Fantasy appears to meet these criteria, in that it can be segmented, proceeds smoothly and rapidly, shows evidence of organization within segments, unfolds through major portions in an automatic and unplanned fashion, is often easily forgotten, and requires little concentrated effort.

As conceived here, integrated response sequences are not necessarily highly sterotyped acts but may incorporate a degree of feedback-using flexibility. Response *schemata* may become integrated, with the specification of a particular act depending on the stimulus supports available for it.

3.6 *Fantasy can occur concurrently with other, nonideational activities or intercurrently with spaced ideational responses.*

Since fantasy makes use of imaginal and verbal responses, it cannot occur simultaneously with other imaginal and verbal activities, or with motor activities that require transformational thought. However, its integrated-response qualities render it compatible with nonideational activity. It has in fact been reported experimentally to occur both concurrently with other kinds of activity and in the interstices of directed cognitive processes.

Consequently, fantasy forms a respondent channel that can unobtrusively express the individual's spontaneous reactions to situations and remind him of his continuing concerns.

3.7   *The span and quality of integration depends on aspects of the subject's physiological state, such as arousal, fatigue, sleep, and pathological conditions.*

"Span of integration" means the length of integrated segments. Extremely fatigued subjects, for instance, find far greater than usual difficulty in executing lengthy integrated sequences of operant behavior. It seems likely—but data are lacking—that segments in fantasy also become shorter.

"Quality of integration" means the accuracy, veridicality, or associative course of an integrated sequence. With fatigue or certain hypnotic drugs, associations become, for instance, increasingly dependent on the sound characteristics instead of the meanings of antecedent words, and integrated sequences make less effective use of feedback, thus permitting the emergence of more idiosyncratic or symbolic behavior.

These considerations lead to two corollary propositions.

3.7.1   *To each physiological state of the human organism there belongs a characteristic form of respondent activity.*

That is, the respondent "baseline" is different waking than sleeping, refreshed than fatigued, excited than relaxed.

3.7.2   *Dream symbolism and other characteristic properties of dream mentation are instances of degenerated forms of integrated sequences.*

Reduction in the organizational complexity of integrated sequences as a result of physiological-state variables is here called "degeneration" of integrated sequences. No value judgment, of course, is intended by the choice of term.

As the span of integration drops, segments become more easily disrupted by competing processes, such as new segments elicited by external or internal stimuli, including stimuli inherent in the segment that becomes disrupted. The content of the new segment may bear little formal resemblance to that of the disrupted segment. The result is here called "sequential fusion."

As the quality of integration changes in the direction of more clang and rebus associations and reduced use of feedback, the plurisignificance of the meaning complexes draws together elements that are poorly coordinated from a reality standpoint, with the result that the fantasy or dream images themselves become increasingly contaminated and bizarre. The result is here called "morphological fusion."

Clearly, the same explanation might well apply to the properties of psychotic thought. It would seem profitable to investigate the response integrations of psychotic patients to ascertain whether the disintegration that is apparent in their ideational activity is detectable also in other aspects of functioning.

4. THE SEQUENCING OF SEGMENTS

4.1 *Disruption of respondent segments and shifts in thematic content are accompanied by whole or vestigial orienting reactions and other affective responses.*

Theories of directed thinking have made use of the notion that shifts in ideational content are interiorized homologues of shifts in perceptual focus. There are so far no hard data to support the extension of perceptual regularities to purely ideational activity, but the proposition is readily testable.

Orienting reactions or their components presumably occur in response to internal stimuli which prominently include the contents of the segment that is disrupted. Thus, respondent segments are in a sense self-disruptive, thereby giving rise to the fractionation described in Proposition 2.6 and to the "drift" in thematic content that is subjectively a prominent feature of fantasy and dreams. The property of self-disruption is not peculiar to respondent segments but is presumably a far more important factor in respondent sequences than in operant sequences, since the latter entail additional feedback controls which respondent sequences are presumed to lack. A disrupted respondent segment may give way either to another respondent or to an operant segment.

4.2 *During the regnancy of a subself, relevant ideational responses are potentiated.*

Evidence exists that aroused affects, drug states, and situational circumstances facilitate the occurrence of related fantasy content, operant responses, and recall.

4.3 *During the regnancy of a subself, irrelevant ideational responses are at least partially suppressed.*

When affective or pharmacological states are induced that are different from those in which certain responses were acquired, the likelihood of their occurrence is lowered and irrelevant fantasy content may be actively suppressed. The evidence for this and the previous proposition comes from a variety of sources, including studies of modeling effects on achievement fantasy, state-dependent learning, experimental "repression," avoidance conditioning, and introspective reports. Since determining that apparent suppression is not simply the absence of potentiation presents some difficult methodological problems, the evidence for active suppression must be considered suggestive but not conclusive.

4.4   *During fantasy activity, when the subselves that are aroused are un-accompanied by related instrumental activity, the regnancy of an aroused subself is short-lived, and a subself that has subsided is replaced by another subself which is thematically different from the preceding one.*

The evidence is contained in experiments that elicited subselves by the use of filmed models in an experimental design capable of assessing some aspects of the rate of change in content. "Short-lived" seemed in that case to be less than 10 to 20 minutes, but the precise duration of a subself's regnancy no doubt depends greatly on parameters that the evidence has not yet begun to specify.

4.5   *The thematic and affective content of respondent segments is capable of instigating operant sequences.*

Conditioning experiments have shown that externally elicited affective states can control the emission of overt operant activity, and introspective reports indicate that spontaneous respondent segments may occasion operant ideational segments.

In this way, respondent processes act as reminders of pressing business other than that in which the individual is momentarily engaged. There is thus a real possibility that for individuals who lead complex occupational lives, who are engaged in numerous current concerns, such as administrators, efficiency is increased up to a point by work situations which permit or encourage the operation of unconstrained respondent processes. Properly spaced periods of relaxation and limitation of the volume of new information input may facilitate this respondent function.

4.6   *Respondent segments may intrude into an operant sequence. The frequency of intrusion is a direct function of the difficulty and duration of operant activity and of sleep loss, and an inverse function of the amount of incentive for uninterrupted operant activity.*

All of these factors that affect the intrusion of respondent segments upon operant sequences have been identified in experimentally manipulated introspective accounts, and the effect of sleep loss is additionally buttressed by behavioral evidence. The precise nature of "difficulty of operant activity" is hard to specify at this juncture, but it appears to be a multidimensional variable of the complexity of the cognitive transformations required by the task and, inversely, the degree to which the subject possesses the requisite skills in integrated form.

The most common instance of the intrusion described here is, of course, "mind-wandering," but there are other instances such as hallucinations, illusions, and motor response errors. In addition, the proposition encompasses the social phenomenon, often encountered in work groups, of collective "punchiness."

The specific susceptibility of hard mental work to interruption by respondent segments suggests a concept of "operant fatigue," in which processes specific to complex operant ideation fatigue independently of other processes and give way to mind-wandering. Casual observation suggests that operant fatigue may occur in the absence of other kinds of fatigue, such as general physical weariness. Under the particularly demanding circumstances of attempting unsuccessfully to solve a complex novel problem, operant fatigue seems to develop especially quickly. In that case, operant fatigue may also bear some relationship to the phenomenon of semantic satiation. When operant processes are progressing smoothly (integratedly?) and successfully, operant fatigue may become less conspicuous than other forms of fatigue. Operant fatigue may well be an adaptive property of the organism, since it is particularly likely to occur when uncreative assaults on a problem are ineffective or inefficient, at which point the intrusion of respondent activity may facilitate a creative solution.

4.7   *Some components of respondent activity continue to occur during operant sequences, even though their conscious ideational components may be partially or wholly suppressed, and they may thus influence the content and course of concurrent operant activity.*

The evidence is entirely clinical or indirect, but the proposition is readily susceptible to experimental test through external manipulations of respondent processes and monitoring of both autonomic and performance variables. For instance, an experimenter could design a work-group-interaction experiment in which he instates conditioned emotional or other associative responses to unobtrusive stimuli and observes the effects of the stimuli on subjects' autonomic responses and task behaviors.

The significance of the process described in the proposition is that it constitutes a contributory mechanism for intuition, interpersonal sensitivity, originality, resourcefulness, clinical judgment, psychotic language, Rogerian congruence, psychoanalytic transference, and other phenomena and constructs.

4.8   *Respondent activity contributes to creative problem-solving as a function of four conditions: (a) the problem-solver's possession of elements of the solution and relevant cognitive skills in his response repertory; (b) the incentive value or emotional importance of solving the problem to the problem-solver, i.e., its strength as a current concern; (c) the provision of opportunities for respondent processes to occur; and (d) the problem-solver's receptivity towards and confidence in his respondent experiences.*

That creative thinking contains respondent-like segments has long been suspected, though poorly documented beyond the level of anecdotal material. Presumably, respondent activity contributes to creative behavior by expanding the amount of time the problem solver spends dealing with the problem, by bringing diverse elements into juxtaposition, thus perhaps revealing novel patterns and relationships, and by extending the range of his reactions to solutions to include "intuitive" responses that may lie outside his conscious conceptual schemata.

The first and fourth of the four conditions have found support in correlational studies of cognitive and personality factors in creativity as well as in studies of the training of creative problem-solving. The other two conditions emerge occasionally from case studies of creative persons or acts and are derived from the present theory but are otherwise unsupported.

The proposition has obvious implications for the design of educational programs, but it also bears on the design of social institutions generally so as to maximize their facilitation of creative living. It suggests that training practices, the control of information flow, job design, work regulations, incentive systems, and architecture might all profitably be reviewed from the standpoint of their effects on respondent processes and hence on creativity.

5. MOTIVATIONAL EFFECTS ON FANTASY

5.1   *Anticipation of an incentive is necessary and sufficient to start behavior directed at attainment of the incentive.*

Proposition 5.1 emerged from a detailed examination of the nature of motivation and the thrust of contemporary evidence regarding it. That one or another form of expectancy of reward is necessary to direct a sequence of operant behavior is recognized by virtually every major theory of motivation. That anticipation of incentives is sufficient to start behavior, even in the absence of drive, and is furthermore necessary to start behavior, even in the presence of drive, constitutes a still controversial assertion but appears to be consistent with recently accumulating evidence.

This formulation recognizes that drives play crucial roles in behavior, in that they are necessary to instigate consummatory behavior, enliven incentives, give rise to drive stimuli which serve as cues for behavior and nag the organism, and increase the level of the organism's readiness to emit motor acts.

5.1.1 *Anticipation of an incentive instates a directive process which persists until goal-attainment or goal-abandonment in influencing the content of behavior.*

This is a corollary of Proposition 5.1. It is a logically necessary deduction, since anticipation need not remain conscious throughout the goal-striving sequence, the sequence may be interrupted by the need for other operant activity and still resume without further external intervention, and some internal process must therefore be capable of both retaining the impetus to goal attainment and periodically reasserting its control over operant behavior until the goal is attained.

The nature of the directive process is still unknown. It is, however, unlikely that its mechanism is purely affective, although affective responses may serve as a source of evaluative feedback, informing the organism of the success with which it is pursuing its goal.

5.1.2 *Current concerns constitute the behavioral manifestation of the directive process instated with the anticipation of incentives.*

"Current concern" has been defined as the state of having started an instrumental, goal-directed sequence which has not been completed but has also not been abandoned. Although the operations for identifying a current concern require some inference, it is in practice easy to specify criteria for either identifying a current concern observationally or for instating one experimentally. The concept of current concern may therefore be regarded as primarily descriptive and behavioral, fundamentally uncommitted to any particular theory of the mechanisms of motivation. However, if Proposition 5.1 is true, then the existence of a current concern must be evidence for the operation of the directive process instated by anticipation of an incentive.

5.2 *Current concerns potentiate respondent segments whose content is related to the concern.*

By potentiation is meant increasing the probability that a certain class of events will occur. The proposition constitutes the major conclusion drawn from reviews of evidence concerning play, dreams, and projective fantasy, comprising studies designed developmentally, experimentally, and correlationally. The mass of evidence and the generality of the concept of current concerns permit certain corollary propositions.

5.2.1   *Anticipation of incentives subsequently potentiates respondent segments whose content is related to the incentives or to the means for obtaining them.*

The content of projective fantasy—principally TAT stories—reflects experimental manipulations of incentives, regardless of whether the experimenter offers explicit material incentives, suggests that experimental activity is relevant to incentives for which the subjects are probably striving outside of the experimental setting, or places subjects in experimental situations which inherently incorporate incentives. Experiments which succeeded in influencing fantasy content can be distinguished from unsuccessful experiments according to whether the TAT stories were written during an incentive manipulation, or whether the stories were written before the instatement of the incentive or after the goal had either been attained or lost or had become irrelevant.

5.2.2   *Fantasy content is an indirect and undependable indicator of enduring motivational dispositions.*

Enduring motivational dispositions are inferred most directly from a subject's tendency to strive after certain kinds of incentives. If a subject is inclined more than other subjects to strive after, for instance, achievement incentives, then at any given moment he has a higher probability of being involved in an achievement concern, which concern would in turn potentiate achievement content in his fantasies. This formulation, however, builds in stochastic links at two different places: the achievement-disposed subject has only an elevated *probability* of being engaged in a current achievement concern, and the concern only *potentiates* achievement fantasy. Hence, the link between enduring motivational dispositions and fantasy is tenuous and the correlations between them may be expected to be low, as they have in fact been.

5.2.2.1   *TAT scores measure motives in the sense that they stochastically reflect current concerns but not in the sense that they directly measure enduring motivational dispositions. Therefore, validity coefficients are likely to be low.*

This proposition is nearly a restatement of the previous one, since most of the evidence concerning motivational effects on fantasy has been produced with the use of TAT stories. The low level of validity that has been found consistently between TAT need scores and other measures of motivation and performance amply support the proposition.

5.2.2.2   *The cyclical, drifting nature of fantasy limits the reliability of TAT scores.*

The tenuous, stochastic link that Proposition 5.2.2 envisages between motivational dispositions and TAT scores, together with the interactions of concerns and picture stimuli, would rule out the possibility of high stability of TAT scores either during a single testing session or from one occasion to the next. Evidence regarding the stability of TAT need scores confirms the proposition.

5.2.3 *Those attributes of incentives that govern the effectiveness with which incentives control operant behavior also govern their capacity to potentiate fantasy content.*

There is no evidence to support the proposition directly. However, if anticipation of incentives indeed governs operant behavior and potentiates related fantasy content, it seems likely that at least some of the same incentive factors govern the intensity of both effects.

5.2.4 *Individuals' social statuses indirectly influence the content of their fantasies.*

Social status imposes corresponding roles on people, whose role behavior is then shaped by the reward matrix in which society imbeds them. Thus, statuses carry with them prescriptions of permissible incentives, which in turn potentiate relevant fantasies. The proposition is consistent with the pattern of available evidence concerning achievement fantasy.

One implication is that insofar as certain role-inappropriate fantasies might contribute to creative thinking about certain kinds of problems, social status limits the areas in which individuals can think creatively.

5.2.5 *Anticipation of incentives influences fantasy content only if the chance of attaining the incentives is to some degree uncertain.*

The effective attractiveness of incentives depends to some extent on their apparent accessibility. An incentive that seems totally inaccessible is effectively not an incentive, and cannot produce a current concern. On the other hand, when attainment of an incentive has become absolutely certain, the instrumental sequence leading to the incentive has terminated successfully, and the concern has in most circumstances ended. The only apparent exceptions are cases in which physiological drive states such as hunger may produce drive stimuli which nag the organism between completion of the instrumental sequence and consummation.

5.2.6 *Apart from their correlations with anticipated incentives, drives as such exert no influence on the content of fantasy.*

There have been few investigations whose procedures separated the operations of drive from those of incentive. In every instance where the two